goof-proof

COLLEGE

ADMISSIONS

ESSAYS

goof-proof COLLEGE ADMISSIONS ESSAYS

Lauren Starkey

LEARNINGEXPRESS ®

NEW YORK

Library of Congress Cataloging-in-Publication Data:
Starkey, Lauren B., 1962–
   Goof-proof college admissions essays / Lauren Starkey.—1st ed.
      p. cm.
Includes bibliographical references (p.   ).
    ISBN 1-57685-470-1
   1. College applications—United States—Handbooks, manual, etc.
   2. Universities and colleges—United States—Admission—Handbooks,
manuals, etc. I. Title.
LB2351.52.U6S73 2003
808'.066378—dc21   2003010397

Printed in the United States of America

9 8 7 6 5 4 3 2 1

First Edition

ISBN 1-57685-470-1

For more information or to place an order, contact LearningExpress at:
   55 Broadway
   8th Floor
   New York, NY 10006

Or visit us at:
   www.learnatest.com

ABOUT THE AUTHOR

Lauren Starkey is a writer and editor, specializing in educational and reference works, with over ten years of experience. For eight years, she worked on the *Oxford English Dictionary*, and she is the author of *Goof-Proof Business Writing, Certified Fitness Instructor Career Starter,* and *Hotel/Restaurant Management Career Starter*. In addition, she has coauthored several career-related books.

CONTENTS

Introduction—Why You Need to Write a Great Essay   xi

SECTION ONE
The Goof-Up—Skipping Important Prewriting Steps   1

Rule #1 Find Your Voice: Journaling   3

Rule #2 Take a Personal Inventory   7

Rule #3 Expand Your Notes   15

Rule #4 Explore the Topics   18

Rule #5 Choose a Topic   22

SECTION TWO
The Goof-Up—Not Writing a Workable Rough Draft   29

Rule #6 Focus Your Topic   31

Rule #7 It's All in the Details   35

Rule #8 Write to Your Audience   38

Rule #9 Write a Compelling Introduction   41

Rule #10 Use the Body of Your Essay Effectively   45

Rule #11 Finish with a Flourish — 48

Rule #12 Watch What You Read — 51

SECTION THREE
The Goof-Up—Writing without Clarity — 55

Rule #13 Make Modifiers Work for You — 56

Rule #14 Be Concise — 58

Rule #15 Eliminate Ambiguity — 61

Rule #16 Avoid Unclear Pronoun References — 63

Rule #17 Avoid Unnecessary Repetition — 65

Rule #18 Think Twice before Opening Your Thesaurus — 67

SECTION FOUR
The Goof-Up—Choosing the Wrong Words — 69

Rule #19 Learn the Most Commonly Confused Words,
and Use Them Properly — 71

Rule #20 Learn the Most Misused Words, and Use
Them Properly — 74

Rule #21 Don't Use Words That Aren't Really Words — 77

Rule #22 Don't Use Words or Phrases That Might
Offend Your Reader — 79

Rule #23 Understand Positive and Negative
Connotations to Choose Words Wisely — 82

Rule #24 Formality versus Informality — 84

Rule #25 Avoid Overly Informal and Overused
Language — 86

SECTION FIVE
The Goof-Up—Misunderstanding the
Basic Mechanics of Writing — 89

Rule #26 Avoid Common Usage Errors with
Parts of Speech — 90

Rule #27 Avoid Dangling Participles and
    Misplaced Modifiers   95

Rule #28 Nouns and Verbs Must Agree in Number   97

Rule #29 Strive to Write in the Active, Rather Than
    the Passive, Voice   99

Rule #30 Avoid Verb Tense Shifts   100

Rule #31 Avoid Double Negatives   101

Rule #32 There Is No Excuse for Spelling Mistakes   103

Rule #33 Use Punctuation Marks Correctly   110

Rule #34 Use Capital Letters Appropriately   117

SECTION SIX

The Goof-Up—Not Revising, Editing, and
Proofreading Your Essay   121

Rule #35 How to Revise   123

Rule #36 How to Edit   131

Rule #37 Professional Revision and Editing Tricks:
    Harnessing the Power of Your Word Processor   137

Rule #38 How to Proofread   142

Rule #39 Professional Proofreading Tricks to
    Catch Spelling Errors   145

SECTION SEVEN

The Goof-Up—Using the Wrong Application   147

Rule #40 The Ins and Outs of Online Submission   149

Rule #41 The Ins and Outs of Mail-In Submission   155

SECTION EIGHT

Resources   161

Appendix A—Online and Print Resources,
Spell- and Grammar-Checking Functions   163

Appendix B—Answer Key   173

WHY YOU NEED TO WRITE A GREAT ESSAY

You can't go back and change your high school grades or recalculate your class rank. You have already taken the SAT exam or ACT assessment, possibly even twice. These scores have been sent to the appropriate places. Your letters of recommendation are done. These are the factors to be considered by the admissions committees that are now set in stone. However, there is still one factor that you have complete control over: your admissions essay.

Why is it so important to write a great essay? There are a number of reasons, the first being that the essay is a critical piece of your application. While it is not considered the most important factor influencing admissions decisions, schools consistently cite it as a highly significant component that is gaining importance every year. In the National Association for College Admission Counseling's (www.nacac.com) annual survey of colleges and universities, recent respondents noted that the essay or writing sample's importance increased, while other factors influencing admissions decisions decreased. That is not to say that your GPA and test scores are less critical, but only that those evaluating your application are weighing essays more heavily than ever before.

Even those schools that state grades and test scores are the most important admissions criteria can end up making application decisions based on the essay. Consider that hundreds, if not thousands, of applicants to the same school will have near identical grades and test scores. How does the admissions committee make their decision? They use the essay as a "tip factor;" all other things being equal, whose essay is better than the rest? In this scenario, your essay can easily become the school's reason for accepting or rejecting your application.

Another reason you need a great essay is if you find that your grades and test scores fall below the median reported by the school to which you are applying. You need *something* on your application that makes you stand out from the crowd, and that makes up for your academic shortcomings. A well-written essay can do just that.

Keep in mind that admissions committees are not just looking for A students, or star athletes. They want a diverse group of people who can bring a variety of talents and personalities to their school. Ron Moss, Director of Enrollment Management at Southern Methodist University, speaks for hundreds of schools when he notes the variety of students he and his admissions committee are looking for:

"We need geniuses in our class to ensure academic pace.

We need an occasional eccentric to balance our cynicism and remind us of our individuality.

We need artists and musicians to represent the richness of our pilgrimage.

We need leaders who can provide vision and inspiration.

We need active members and doers who can make the vision come true.

We need athletes and 4-H'ers and math whizzes and ultimate Frisbee and quiz bowl champs, and travelers of foreign lands, and givers of themselves."

Source: www.mycollegeguide.org/read/real.html

How can you write a college admissions essay or a personal statement that is not just the best writing you are capable of, but one that will improve your chances of college admissions? This book guides you through the process by breaking down the project into manageable rules to follow, giving you step-by-step instructions, and providing you with examples taken from real essays and tips from those in the admissions field.

● HOW THE GOOF-PROOF METHOD WORKS ●

The 41 Goof-Proof Rules are presented in Goof-Up form. You will read about a common mistake, then learn how to Goof-Proof yourself, or avoid the mistake. *Goof-Proof College Admissions Essays* covers everything you need to know to write a winning essay including:

- examining your life and experiences for material to write about
- choosing an essay topic that best presents you and your story
- focusing and organizing your content
- writing to your audience
- composing a workable rough draft
- clarifying your writing
- choosing the right words to get your point across

Writing well also means following the rules of grammar and spelling. Although most college essays are written on a computer with grammar and spell checkers, these high-tech helpers aren't goof-proof. You still need to know basic mechanics in order to write well. The nine Goof-Proof Rules of mechanics detailed in Section Five explain simply and directly the information you need to know.

The book is divided into seven parts, each covering a different aspect of the essay writing process:

- **Section One:** Explains the benefits and how-to's of exploring possible content and topics for your essay.

- **Section Two:** Teaches you how to write a rough draft by using an outline and adding the right kinds of details to best reach your audience.
- **Section Three:** Is all about clarity. You will determine exactly what you want to say and how to say it in the most direct, specific, and unambiguous way.
- **Section Four:** Examines the importance of word choice. You will learn how to correctly use the most confused and misused words, and how to avoid alienating or baffling your reader through improper word choices.
- **Section Five:** Is a review of writing basics. The parts of speech and common grammatical errors are explained and made goof-proof. Spelling, punctuation marks, and capitalization are also covered.
- **Section Six:** Shows you how to revise, edit, and proofread your essay. Professional editing and proofreading tips are included to help bring your essay into final form.
- **Section Seven:** Explains the pros and cons of traditional paper applications and online versions, and gives you tips for improving your application no matter which format you choose.
- **Section Eight:** Appendix A contains resource material, such as online application websites, more writing, grammar, and spelling resources, and information on how to take full advantage of your computer's formatting, grammar, and spelling tools. Appendix B is where you will find the answer keys to the eleven quizzes throughout the book.

There is no other essay resource, either in print or online, that contains all of the information gathered in *Goof-Proof College Admissions Essays*. We have done our homework. Now, it's time for you to do yours: Read on and get ready to write your college admissions essay.

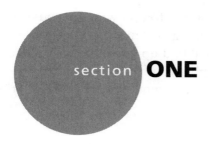

section **ONE**

THE GOOF–UP:
SKIPPING IMPORTANT
PREWRITING STEPS

The college essay is a critical part of your application. A good one can help make up for grades and test scores that aren't as high as you would like them to be. A memorable essay can also make you stand out from a crowd of equally eligible applicants. It can easily become the admissions committee's reason for accepting or rejecting your application.

Such an important document is worth taking your time over. Don't simply choose a topic at random and begin writing. There is a process to putting together a great essay, and following it can mean the difference between acceptance and rejection. The first step in the process is prewriting, which involves exploring possible content (what you might write about) and the topics on your applications (the subjects you might address).

Begin with the Goof-Proof Rules for journaling and personal inventory, which help you to collect the raw data from which you can create one or more personal statements. Look at the topics available, and learn great ways to approach each one. "Try on" a number of them to find the best fit. Then, create notes from which you can write your essay.

By following the Goof-Proof Rules for prewriting, you will learn to use your time wisely, getting organized before you sit down to write. That means you will end up with a better college application essay, one that highlights your strengths and experiences in the personal style admissions committees are looking for.

RULE #1: Find Your Voice: Journaling

Your personal statement should be written in your own voice.

● **GOOF-PROOF IT!** ●

You will hear it everywhere you look for college essay writing advice: Write your personal statement in your own voice. But what does that mean exactly? You have a voice you use with your friends, another with your teachers, and still another with your parents and family. Which one is right for your essay?

Using the information in this book well ahead of time will give you an advantage. You will have more time to find great material to write about and to understand how to translate that material into a winning essay. The first step is to start keeping a journal.

If you are like many busy students, your first reaction may be, "who has time for journal writing?" Or, this advice may seem unrelated to the major task you have to accomplish. But it is actually the best method for beginning your essay, for two important reasons.

1. Your journal will sound like you, written in an authentic voice that should need very few adjustments when applied to the essay.
2. Your journal can be a great source for ideas. You can write about what's important to you, your goals and aspirations, your values, or your take on everything from popular culture to current events.

Journaling doesn't have to be elaborate, or time consuming. Take a minimum of five minutes a day to write or type something personal. In order to journal successfully, you will need to make it a habit. In order to do that, you need to make the process as simple and painless as possible. Think about your habits, and which of these two journaling options best suit you. You can write in a book you have designated as your journal, or you can make journal entries on your computer, either in word processing documents, or in one of the many new online journal sites.

Goof-Proof Advice from the Experts

Rachel Klein, a college counselor at Milton Academy in Milton, Massachusetts, advises her students to keep journals to help with essay writing because they can "give them back their own words." Journals, Klein says, are like "your mind coming out on paper." When you are writing your essay, you can use the journal as a reference for tone and word choices that convey your authentic voice.

If you are writing, get a journal that is small enough to carry with you everywhere you go. When inspiration hits, you will be ready. Can't get started? Pick a time and place to write in your journal each day. If you are typing, set aside a specific time to journal. Open your journal document before going online to avoid distractions and stick with it for the allotted time period.

If you are considering an online journal, visit www.blogger.com and www.livejournal.com to see how they are set up. Some sites require you to type entries while online, and others have downloadable diaries that may be added to at any time. A potential problem with these types of sites is the distractions. There are other diarist's entries to read, software to play around with, and features such as uploading pictures that can keep you from your real task. If you can't get right down to work, choose a handwritten or simple word processing journal.

Try some of the Goof-Proof Journal Prompts on the next page to shake up an existing journal, or get you started on a new one. If you are new to journaling, find some paper, or open a word processor document, and write about yourself, the world as you see it, or something that happened today. The subjects are limitless, but remember to keep it about *you*. These prompts can help you if you are stuck, if you want some direction for your writing, or they can even trigger a unique idea.

● GOOF-PROOF EXAMPLE ●
JOURNAL PROMPTS

- Write a letter to someone who has had a significant influence on you. Use as many details as possible to *show,* rather than *tell,* why they are so important to you.
- Choose a current event, and discuss its importance to you. Be as personal as possible: How has the event changed your thinking? How does it make you feel? How has it impacted your daily life or your future plans?
- Describe a risk you took, and what you gained or lost by taking it. Did you learn something about yourself or the world? Are you a "different" person because you took the risk? Was it worth it?
- Choose a work of creativity (visual, musical, literary, scientific) that is of particular importance to you. How has it influenced you? Describe it in great detail, and remember to keep it personal.
- Have you had a travel experience that affected you somehow? Recount the experience as specifically as possible, using the five senses to detail it.
- Describe a ritual you perform often that has meaning to you. Think small. Do you meditate when you wake up in the morning? Listen to a certain kind of music while studying or reading? Cook something for yourself when you are stressed out? Don't worry if the ritual is quirky, or one that won't seem important to someone else.
- Imagine a perfect world. What does "perfect" mean to you? Get as detailed as possible. Aside from the requisite world peace and clean environment, think about the day-to-day things that would make a difference to you. Would every coffee maker have a "pause and serve" feature? Would the Dave Matthews Band perform free concerts at your school every Saturday? Would everyone in your state, upon getting their driver's license, be given the car of their choice?

Once you begin the essay writing stage, your journal will become an invaluable tool. It can help you use the right tone, neither too casual nor too formal, so that your essay sounds like you. While rereading it, make note of the words you use, and what your voice sounds like when you write. Also make note of the ideas and topics that hold your interest. Sometimes you may not be aware of your feelings about something until you take the time to explore them. Use your journal entries to search for possible essay material.

RULE #2: Take a Personal Inventory

Taking a personal inventory will help you come up with an idea to write about in your essay.

● GOOF-PROOF IT! ●

The personal inventory helps you catalogue possible subjects, inspiring you to think about your life in new ways as material for your writing. In short, this cataloguing tool is designed to help you mine your life for raw material that you can use in your essay. Although you won't use all, or even most of the information you gather, be willing to explore many possibilities before narrowing down your essay topic. It will be useful when filling out the rest of your application, too.

● GOOF-PROOF RULE OF THUMB ●
WHAT ADMISSIONS OFFICERS ARE LOOKING FOR

Although you do want to include as much information as possible, keep in mind a number of important qualities that admissions officers are looking for. How do we know what those are? Take a look at the blank recommendation forms you will hand out to your teachers. The admissions committee asks them to rate you in:

creative, original thought	intellectual ability
motivation	academic achievement
self confidence	written expression of ideas
independence	disciplined work habits
initiative	potential for growth

What activities and experiences can you write about that highlight one or more of these? How can you show (rather than tell) in your essay that you have these qualities? Keep them in mind when filling out your inventory.

● GOOF-PROOF PRACTICE ●

To complete the personal inventory, use the following pages to fill in your information in the appropriate areas.

1. *History*

   Think back to your earliest memory, and go from there. Move chronologically, cataloguing events in your life, until you reach the most recent one(s). Don't limit yourself to dramatic or life-altering experiences. Spend the most time on the past few years, unless you already know you will write about an event in your childhood.

   _____

   _____

   _____

   _____

   _____

   _____

   _____

   _____

   _____

   _____

   _____

   _____

   _____

   _____

   _____

2. *Achievements and Accomplishments*

List all awards or other commendations you have received (academic, extra-curricular, and so on). Also include goals you have reached or accomplished, that may not have been recognized by others. What has been important to you and your personal growth? What achievements are you most proud of?

_____

_____

_____

_____

_____

_____

_____

_____

_____

_____

_____

_____

_____

_____

_____

_____

_____

3. *Activities*

Outside the classroom, what have you spent your time doing? These may be one-time or on-going. Keep in mind, but don't limit yourself to: sports, civic groups, travel, volunteer work, art projects, technology, or religious groups. Why did you start each activity, and, if applicable, why do you continue with it? Remember, many of these are listed in other places on your application. Think about things you have done that are not mentioned elsewhere, or not given significant attention on the rest of the application. You may use your essay to highlight these accomplishments.

_____

_____

_____

_____

_____

_____

_____

_____

_____

_____

_____

_____

_____

4. *Influences*

Make a list of the people, events, works of art, literature, and music that have affected you in a meaningful way.

_____

_____

_____

_____

_____

_____

_____

_____

_____

_____

_____

_____

_____

_____

_____

_____

_____

_____

5. *Skills*

What are you good at? You may want to ask friends and family members to help with this. Skills may be those acquired through learning and practice, such as playing an instrument, or personal attributes, such as leadership or willingness to follow the road less traveled.

_____

_____

_____

_____

_____

_____

_____

_____

_____

_____

_____

_____

_____

_____

_____

6. *Passions*

What makes your blood boil or your heart beat faster? Is there a sports team you follow with fervor, a book you have read ten times, or a topic of local, national, or global importance that gets you riled up? You may have listed these already in other sections; repeat them here because this category examines them from a different point of view.

_____

_____

_____

_____

_____

_____

_____

_____

_____

_____

_____

_____

_____

_____

RULE #3: Expand Your Notes

Make the "skeleton" of your inventory come to life. Flesh it out with details, anecdotes, memories, and dialogue.

● **GOOF-PROOF IT!** ●

As you read your completed inventory, add notes or details to everything you have written. For some items, you may only add a word or two. For others, you might be inspired to add a paragraph or more. The more details you add, the better. If you need to add a fresh sheet of paper, go ahead and keep writing. Be as specific as possible. For example, it wasn't just a test, it the final exam of the term—and you needed an A to pass! It wasn't just a game, it was the last game of the season, against your school's arch rival. It may take you an hour or more to expand your notes, but this exercise is critical in helping determine which topic to select, and how best to approach it.

Look for patterns in your notes, or topics that are repeated in two or more areas on the inventory. How do your skills connect with your activities or passions? Perhaps you didn't think of science as a guiding force in your life, but now you see you have listed your physics teacher as a major influence, learning about the space program as a passion, and the astronomy club as your favorite activity. Link any like items together with different colored highlighters, or draw lines that connect them.

Choose two items from your notes that you could tell a story about. Write two or three paragraphs for each. Then answer: Why did you tell it? What does it say about who you are? As you expand your notes through these exercises, you may begin to see what is most interesting and useful to write about in your essay. Keep your notes in mind as you explore the various topics your applications present for you to choose from.

● GOOF-PROOF EXAMPLE ●
CONNECTIONS FROM NOTES

Passions: Desire to be a marine biologist (love the
    water, wildlife, studying science)
History: Class trip to Belize (began to think about
    marine biology as career)
Activities: scuba diving class
Influence: Dr. Nancy Foster, head of the National
    Ocean Service
Achievements: Science Department Award, Junior
    year

My trip to Belize last year with my science class convinced me that my dream of becoming a marine biologist could become a reality. Studying the marine
ecosystem was fascinating, and I want to learn more
and make it my life's work. I am inspired by the life of
Dr. Nancy Foster, who did so much to address the problems of habitat destruction and conservation.

● GOOF-PROOF PRACTICE ●

Use this space to make connections from your notes.

_____

_____

_____

_____

_____

_____

_____

_____

_____

_____

_____

_____

_____

_____

_____

_____

_____

_____

_____

_____

_____

_____

_____

_____

_____

_____

RULE #4: Explore the Topics

Understand what each topic is about, and how to best approach it, before making a selection.

• GOOF-PROOF IT! •

Most applications offer at least two essay topics. The Common Application (see Section Seven) has five. Keep an open mind as you explore the topics you have to choose from. While you could write a decent essay on many of them, there is probably one that allows you to present yourself best in a truly great and original way.

If you are applying to one or more of the 230 schools that accept the Common Application, you will have five topics to choose from. Other colleges and universities use their own topics, which are similar to the ones found on the Common Application. All of the topics are designed to make you write in a highly personal way about yourself, and therefore, give the admissions committee more information on which to base their decision.

• GOOF PROOF EXAMPLE •
COMMON APPLICATION ESSAY TOPICS

1. *Evaluate a significant experience, achievement, risk you have taken, or ethical dilemma you have faced, and its impact on you.*

    The last phrase is critical: Whatever you choose to write about (the "cause"), you must show its impact upon you (the "effect"). Your experience need not be earth-shattering; remember that small and seemingly insignificant can be better: You are guaranteed to write an original essay if you focus on something that you alone experienced or find significance in.

    Writing an essay on, for instance, what it felt like to drive a car alone for the first time, or why you enjoy preparing a favorite recipe, can show your creativity and your willingness to see the big picture. Perhaps the cooking experience showed you how a bunch of little steps add up to something big, or how a series of words on paper can connect you with your ethnic heritage. In other words, they don't want to know about how you took first prize in the Mozart Piano Competition. If you want to write about piano playing, you could briefly mention winning the prize, but explain how the rigors of practice, the wisdom of your teacher, and the knowledge of musical composition have changed you for the better.

2. *Discuss some issue of personal, local, national, or international concern and its importance to you.*

Many experts caution against writing on this topic unless the issue has had a profound and highly personal effect on you. It lends itself to clichés ("why I want world peace") and can steer you away from your task, which is to reveal something about yourself. Another potential problem with this topic is that you can alienate yourself from your reader. You don't know if your essay will be read by a 20-something, a 70-something, Democrat or Republican, male or female, married or single, liberal or conservative. Be careful not to dismiss or critique the other side of your argument while laying out your own. Since this topic is not among the most popular, you may stand out simply by choosing it. Just avoid the potential problems, and display your knowledge of the issue, while keeping the focus highly personal.

3. *Indicate a person who has had a significant influence on you, and describe that influence.*

Be wary of choosing a famous person as an influence. The admissions officers have read many essays about Martin Luther King, Mother Theresa, and Charles Lindbergh. If you write about a famous person, you need to get highly creative in your explanation of *how* he or she influenced you. Successful essays on this topic typically center on someone known personally to the writer (although be aware that parents are favorites with many essay writers, meaning again that you will need to be highly creative in order to write a unique essay). No matter who you write about, remember that the question is a catalyst for revealing information about you, not about your role model. Don't simply describe the person. Show evidence of yourself throughout your essay by relating everything back to you.

4. *Describe a character in fiction, an historical figure, or a creative work (as in art, music, science, etc.) that has had an influence on you.*

    As with number three, you need to keep the focus on *you,* not the character or creative work. Your choice of topic does reveal something about you, but you need to reveal even more by showing how she/he/it has influenced you. This is not one of the most popular topics, so you will have a good chance of standing out just by choosing it. Just be certain to keep it personal.

5. *Topic of your choice.*

    This question is found on dozens of applications (other than the Common one) in many different forms. Massachusetts Institute of Technology asks, "We want to get to know you as a person. Make up a question that is personally relevant to you, state it clearly, and answer it. Feel free to use your imagination, recognizing that those who read it will not mind being entertained." Seton Hall University puts it this way: "The application lists several topic suggestions, but feel free to write about any subject that you feel is relevant and will enable us to get to know you." As with the request for a writing sample below, this topic lends itself to essay "recycling." If you already have a well-written, vivid piece on something of great significance to you, something you know well, and that has changed or greatly impacted upon you, you may use it here.

• TWO OTHER POPULAR PROMPTS •
WITH SUGGESTED APPROACHES

1. *Why are you applying to our school?*

What they want to hear: that you will attend if they accept you, that you will graduate from their school, and that you have something meaningful to contribute to the school community. This question requires research using resources other than the website and brochures or other published material generated by the school. Are there alumni or current students in your area? Talk to them about what the school is really like, and use this material to highlight your unique personality. Does the school host an international science fair every year? Mention it if you are dying to meet and speak with a renowned scientist who frequently attends. Does the literary magazine win top honors at the national level? Include some of your poetry and write about your dream of getting published and working in the publishing industry.

2. *Submit a writing sample.*

There are three ways to approach this, two of which can save you time by "recycling" essays you have already written. The first is, of course, to write a new essay specifically for the application, but that option doesn't make much sense when you probably have appropriate samples already written.

You may also submit the original copy of an essay you wrote for a class, with teacher comments. Be certain to use an essay that got an A, and is on an interesting topic. The advantages to this choice are that it is fast, and it effectively gives you another teacher recommendation if the comments are positive, (particularly if he or she didn't already write one of your recommendations). You may also submit a rewrite of an essay written for a class, improving it by incorporating teacher comments (which in effect gives you the use of an editor). There is no need to mention the grade the essay received, or the class or teacher it was required by.

RULE #5: Choose a Topic

The sooner you choose your topic, the sooner you can start shaping your essay.

● GOOF-PROOF IT! ●

You have learned about each topic, how best to approach it, and what it may reveal about you. Now, brainstorm possible answers. Evaluate your notes to find the topic that will best highlight your strengths and unique personality.

This is probably the most difficult and important part of the application process, but prewriting and brainstorming are a great help. Once you "try on" each topic, it will become clear which one(s) allows you to present yourself and your story best. Which one can you make the best emotional connection with? That's the one that will connect with your readers, too.

Goof-Proof Advice from the Experts

College counselor Dr. Beverly Lenny advises students to "choose the right vehicle to express yourself. What you want to say is more important than the question itself."

Go back over the topics from Rule #4, adding any other topics your applications may provide you with. Then:

1. For each different topic or question, use a separate sheet of paper, and write the topic at the top.
2. Write anything that comes to mind in response to that topic. Your ideas may be in the form of a neat list, moving from the most to least important, or they can be random, needing more organization later.
3. Get out your personal inventory, and match information with the topics. Do your summer job at the local independent bookstore and all you have learned from your

eccentric boss fit well with topic #3? What about your obsession with fashion photography? It could be narrowed down to a specific creative work or body of work (topic #4); it could also work well as a significant experience (topic #1) if you write about your visit to New York to attend a seminar at the Fashion Institute of Technology.

● GOOF-PROOF CHECKLIST ●

Once you have prewriting notes on each topic, answer the following:

✓ Can I answer the question or address the topic completely?
✓ Does the topic let me highlight something about myself that wasn't evident on the rest of the application?
✓ Is the topic about something personally significant and important to my life?
✓ Can I make the essay unique, easily avoiding clichés?
✓ Will my essay on this topic tell the committee something they will like about me?
✓ Can I write about myself and this topic without bragging or overstating my importance?
✓ Will my essay on this topic hold the interest of the reader?
✓ Does the topic avoid potentially offensive subjects?

● Making the Choice

For most students, it is becoming clear at this point which topic best suits their life, strengths, and experiences, lending itself to the most unique and insightful essay. However, if more than one topic seems like a good fit, go back to your inventory. Using a different colored highlighter for each topic, mark the information that could be used to write on that topic. To which topic can you bring the most actual experiences and concrete details?

Goof-Proof Advice from Your Peers

Still not sure? Consider outlining and writing rough drafts of two essays. High school senior Liz Abernathey says she wrote four essays on different topics before coming up with one she liked. "After I wrote the first one, I reread it, and realized that I had told a memory of something I really liked, but nothing more. Rather than trying to fix it, I simply began again. I wrote another essay a few days later, and a similar thing occurred. After reading it, I just didn't feel a "click." This process happened until my fourth essay. Although I only had a rough draft, I knew I had hit upon something good. I felt the click. It just worked better than the other topics."

● GOOF-PROOF EXAMPLE ●
TWO SAMPLE DRAFTS

Indicate a person who has had a significant influence on you, and describe that influence.

When my science teacher assigned a research paper on a scientist of our choice, I wasn't thrilled. I had no one in mind for the month-long project. I sat at the keyboard in the school library, looking for inspiration. Finally, I started a search for "women scientists." I found a hit with a quote from Al Gore, calling the mystery person "an outstanding role model for women scientists across America."

Who was she? The late Dr. Nancy Foster, former Assistant Administrator for Oceanic Services and Coastal Zone Management at the National Oceanic and Atmospheric Administration, and Director of the National Ocean Service. The more I read about this brilliant, dynamic woman, the more I became inspired. Not only did I feel impressed and proud of her many accomplishments, but her story made me think that I could take my love of the ocean and its creatures and make it into a career as a marine biologist.

Evaluate a significant experience, achievement, risk you have taken, or ethical dilemma you have faced, and its impact on you.

When my science teacher suggested a class trip to Belize to study the marine ecosystem, I was excited. The thought of escaping the cold New England winter for sun and sand was my first thought. Then, I wondered if I would be able to go SCUBA diving there, in a real ocean, after four months of taking classes in the chilly pool at the local YMCA. Mr. Carlson told us that we would be making trips to the coral reef in Ambergris Caye and writing up our findings as a report once we got back to school. I didn't know yet that the trip would begin to give direction to my life.

● GOOF-PROOF EXAMPLE ●
TOPICS THAT WORK

- Academic interests if you are passionate about them, such as why you love calculus, the works of Stephen Crane, or studying about the Civil War.
- Anything personal that steers away from a "common mistake." Write about an emotional reaction to an event, a work of art, or another person.
- Success out of failure: What problem did you face that helped you learn a great lesson and grow as a person? How did you turn an obstacle into an attribute or achievement? (But keep it positive; you don't want your essay to sound like a sob story or an excuse for something).

- Small is fine. Most students in their late teens have not experienced a traumatic, life-changing event. Write about something you know about or of great significance to you that might seem mundane or routine to everyone else.
- Something that gets you excited, or something you are passionate about.

● AVOID THE MOST COMMON ESSAY GOOF-UPS ●

Admissions directors note that the worst essays usually fall into one (or more) of three categories:

1. depressing
2. paint an unflattering picture of the applicant
3. are completely impersonal or unoriginal

While just about any experience can be the basis of a great essay, keep in mind the following Goof-Proof tips to avoid committing one of the common blunders:

- **Positive is probably better.** You could write a superb essay on the anxiety you have experienced as a teen (think cliché) or your struggle with depression, but think about your audience. How many times does an admissions officer want to read depressing topics?
- **Think recent past.** They want to know about who you are today, not about your early childhood. Unless it has significant relevance to who you are today, skip it.
- **Keep unflattering experiences to yourself.** You want the admissions officers to like you. Don't tell them about major mistakes or stupid things you did. You want to sound competent and responsible.
- **Avoid overused topics.** Topics such as "world peace," "the impact of my volunteer position," "how my friend's death taught me to enjoy life more," and "teen angst" have all been done before, many times. Unless your take on a popular topic is highly original, and highly personal, you run the risk

of boring your audience. Showcase your uniqueness by steering clear of the more obvious topics and content.

- **Think local, not global.** Large societal or political issues are usually not personal. Subjects such as Middle East peace, September 11, and Columbine have been expounded upon by experts in the media, and you probably don't have a unique perspective (unless you were personally involved or personally impacted). Think specific and personal, rather than abstract and far away from your everyday life.
- **Resist any temptation to brag.** Don't go overboard highlighting your achievements, and especially don't take credit for something you shouldn't. For example, did your team really win the state championship because of your leadership skills? There is a great difference between advocating for yourself and sounding pompous.

● PUTTING IT ALL TOGETHER ●

Your college admissions essay is a critical element in your quest for acceptance at the college of your choice. Don't rush into writing it. Follow the Goof-Proof Rules of essay prewriting to find great material to write about, the right topic to address and the organization that best represents you in your essay. Time spent prewriting translates into a better final product.

● GOOF-PROOF GUIDELINES ●

- Start or continue with journal writing; it is an excellent tool for putting you in touch with your authentic voice.
- Fill out a personal inventory that encourages you to mine your life and experiences for the raw material you will draw on to write your essay.
- Explore the given topics carefully; understand what they are asking for, and how to respond best.

- Compare your notes and inventory to your possible topics. Find the best fit by trying on a number of topics with the material you want to write about.
- Avoid the common mistakes admissions committees don't want to see by following the Goof-Proof Rules.
- Choose a topic that will allow you to best present yourself and your story.

THE GOOF–UP:
NOT WRITING A WORKABLE
ROUGH DRAFT

This section guides you through the process of writing a rough draft. Using the notes and personal inventory you created in Section One, you will arrange and rearrange your material to find the best way to present it. An outline can help by showing the progression from one idea to the next. If it doesn't make sense one way, you can change the pieces around to work better as a whole.

You will learn how to use detail to add interest and vitality to your writing. Sights, sounds, examples, and evidence help your reader to connect with your essay. They also turn a weak essay into a strong one. Details are just one way to draw a positive impression from the admissions committee. Understand who they are and what they are looking for so you can write to your audience and make a connection.

Since admissions officers are assigned hundreds of essays to read, they spend just a few minutes on each one. Use every word wisely. Don't waste time introducing your essay, but rather jump right into it. A dynamic introduction draws the reader in immediately, and acts as a hook that makes your audience want to keep reading. Be certain the body of your essay flows logically from one point to the next, and don't bore your reader or waste his or her time by providing a summary of your essay as a conclusion.

By following the Goof-Proof Rules for writing a rough draft, you will end up with a piece of writing that you can polish into final form and attach to your application with confidence.

RULE #6: Focus Your Topic

When you are clear about the content of your essay and how best to present it, you will write on point, without going off on a tangent or otherwise wasting your reader's time.

● GOOF-PROOF IT! ●

Before you actually begin writing, take the time to clarify the point you are trying to make. The more precise you can be about what you wish to achieve with your essay, the better you will communicate that information to your audience.

Many writers benefit from creating an outline; it helps you to see how your points work together, whether there is a flow or logical progression from one point to the next, and if you need more details or other information.

Creating an outline begins with a reading of your personal inventory and prewriting notes. First, group related ideas together, looking for major topics (which can be headings), and minor ones (which can be subheadings, examples, or details). Define your major points and rearrange them until they make sense and follow a logical progression. You will be able to see the relationships between your ideas as you outline them and determine their importance (major point, minor point, example, detail). If you need more supporting details or facts—subcategories—you can add them now.

● GOOF-PROOF RULE OF THUMB ●
OUTLINE IT

As you outline your information, you can either create topic headings that summarize your main point or write out full sentences for each point on your outline.

● GOOF-PROOF EXAMPLE ●
STANDARD OUTLINE

A standard outline form using Roman and Arabic numerals and upper and lower case letters looks like this:

I.
   A.
      1.
      2.
   B.
      1.
      2.
         a.
         b.

● GOOF-PROOF EXAMPLE ●
OUTLINING YOUR ESSAY

In this excerpt, the writer decided to shape her story as an answer to a prevailing question, which she poses in the introduction: What is she going to do when she graduates? She successfully completes this task by detailing the events in her life, which clearly depict why she wants to pursue teaching, and why she would be a good teacher. The student writer meshes her professional aspirations with personal work experiences using colorful examples. She organizes her story by using each paragraph to describe a different experience, each of which conveys her initially stated goal—to become a teacher.

I.   What am I going to do when I graduate high school?
   A. Others believe I would be a good teacher
   B. I have an inclination towards working with children
   C. I have fond memories of my own childhood

II. High school work experience
   A. Tutored underserved third graders
   B. Created a fictional character for the children, Mijo
   C. Children confided in Mijo and wrote him notes
   D. This was an excellent way to get the children to improve their writing skills
   E. Mijo wrote notes back to the students with encouraging remarks
   F. The creation of Mijo let me know the children better, and let me help them more
III. Challenge in the classroom
   A. Working with poorly disciplined students
   B. Realize need for a solution
   C. Incorporate series of team-building activities to attempt a more productive classroom
   D. The classroom environment is shaping up
IV. Motivations, goals, and final testimony
   A. Challenge of teaching is exciting
   B. Desire to be active participant in the process
   C. Want to better understand educational system
   D. I want to see the results of my teaching—better students

The successful essay written using this outline appears in Section Six.

● GOOF-PROOF CHECKLIST ●

Once you have completed your outline, revise and refine it by following these steps:

✓ Write down your overall goal for your essay. What are you trying to tell the admissions committee about yourself that the rest of your application didn't reveal?

✓ Read through your outline and circle, underline, or highlight your major points or images. Do they all support your goal?

✓ Brainstorm words and phrases that will accurately and concisely express those points. (You may jot them down in the margin of your outline, or use a separate sheet.)

✓ Use this list and your outline to guide your writing. Don't allow yourself to stray from your goal or your major points.

RULE #7: It's All in the Details

The best way to make your essay stand out, and make your point clearly and vividly, is to use details.

● GOOF-PROOF IT! ●

Details are important for your essay because they help the reader connect with your writing. They often involve the senses. You might describe a scene or an object with such clarity that your reader can almost *see* it. Or, you might use dialogue or sounds to help your reader *hear* your essay. Adding detail is important in almost any kind of writing, but it is crucial in the personal essay. The addition of details can turn a weak essay into a winner.

If you haven't started writing, think about details as you develop your notes and outline. For every point you make, come up with three or four details about it. Get as specific as possible.

● GOOF-PROOF EXAMPLE ●
BE SPECIFIC!

We lived in a house.

We lived in a typical center-hall colonial.

We lived in a typical, middle-class, subdivision house: the center-hall colonial.

Details are also instances and examples. Don't just say you love the Harry Potter series by J.K. Rowling. Show it, instead, by describing where and when you bought your first copy of *Harry Potter and the Sorcerer's Stone,* or how you missed soccer practice because you were caught up with reading *Harry Potter and the Order of the Phoenix* and forgot the time. Scenarios that illustrate your point are also great details. Take your reader to your jazz band performance by setting the scene. Describe the festival stage, the crowd, or even the weather.

Specific evidence, such as the exact temperature of the ocean, or statistics, such as how many volunteers you were up against when you won the "Volunteer of the Year" award, are also great details. By being precise, you draw your reader into further identification with your writing. And since your goal is to submit an essay that connects with at least one person on the admissions committee, use as many colorful, relevant details as possible. Remember, dialogue makes a great detail, too.

The only possible drawback of using details is when they aren't really related to your message. Whenever you write about an experience or give some other specific information, have a good reason for its inclusion. Don't leave it up to your reader to draw conclusions or figure out connections. Explain the significance of your material, show how it changed you, or what it meant to you. Review Rule #6 to see how to test your details to be certain they support your essay.

● GOOF-PROOF EXAMPLE ●
VAGUE AND DETAILED SENTENCES

Here are some sentences that leave the reader with a vague sense of understanding, followed by examples of how details can be used effectively:

Vague: I spent the summer working at a store.
Detailed: Eight hours a day, five days a week, I worked at SmartMart last summer, dreaming of the sun that would be setting as I punched out.

Vague: Math is my favorite subject.
Detailed: Calculus made me think in ways I never had before and made me realize that I wanted to follow a career path that involves mathematics.

Vague: I really want to attend XYZ University.
Detailed: The two most important reasons for my decision to apply to XYZ University are its relationship to its inner city community and the quality of the teaching staff in the Economics Department.

Vague: Playing varsity baseball has taught me how to be part of a team.
Detailed: I learned many lessons from my teammates during my three years playing varsity baseball.

RULE #8: Write to Your Audience

It's not easy to describe typical admissions directors. Most schools hire a mix of young and old, scholar and jock, alumni and not, conservative and liberal.

● GOOF-PROOF IT! ●

College admissions committees are usually made up of between ten and twenty people. There is a Dean, or Director of Admissions, who leads a team of Assistant or Associate Directors. Some schools even hire senior interns, who are still working toward their degrees, to evaluate applications. What they have in common is an ability to spot good writing, and a willingness to make a connection with their applicants. Your job is to try to appeal to one or more of them. Remember these facts about admissions committees as you sit down to write your essay.

● GOOF-PROOF CHECKLIST ●

✓ **Keep a diverse audience in mind.** The committees vary a great deal in their composition. Most schools now attempt to provide a diverse group, employing women and minorities.

✓ **Take the initiative to meet your audience.** If you do meet the admissions committee, you can fine-tune your essay to suit their specific requirements and preferences. Typically, each admissions director is in charge of a geographical area of the country, or of the world if the school draws or wants to draw international students. They travel to those areas to attend college fairs, conduct interviews, and speak at secondary schools. They are available to applicants to answer questions and provide a better idea of what the school is like (especially if they are an alumni/ae).

✓ **Grab your audience's attention—quickly!** When applications are submitted, the work of the committee goes into high gear. Some schools receive thousands of applications for a few hundred spots. Others are less selective, but still must evaluate each application they receive. Everyone on the committee gets hundreds of essays to evaluate, meaning they spend an average of two to three minutes reading each one.

✓ **Be yourself.** Admissions directors do not read with a highly judgmental eye, ready to circle every dangling participle or toss your essay if they find an unclear pronoun reference. Instead, they read to find essays that they connect with. The connection is a feeling he or she gets from your writing. It can be that they sense, through your writing skills, that you are capable of a college workload.

Remember, the essay is also referred to as a *personal statement*. The most important connection you can make is not between your reader and the intellectual argument you present, but rather an emotional or personal connection with the content of your essay. Simply put, a winning essay makes admissions directors like you.

● **GOOF-PROOF RULE OF THUMB** ●
SHOULD YOU USE HUMOR?

This is a tough question, and the simple answer is, probably not. A light-hearted, witty tone is fine if it fits with your subject. But resist the urge to tell a wild and crazy story, or to tell a straight one with jokes and puns thrown in. You don't know the sense of humor of your reader. If he or she doesn't find it funny, you run the risk of looking foolish at best. Unless you are known for your great sense of humor, keep your tone upbeat, but leave out the jokes.

Goof-Proof Advice from the Experts

The story goes that college admissions committees love well-rounded students, those who can achieve good grades, play on a varsity team or three, sing in the church choir, and volunteer at the local soup kitchen once a week. They look for applicants who have to staple additional pages into their applications to list all of their extra-curricular activities.

The reality is quite different. Many admissions directors have spoken out about the fact that they are *not* looking for kids who can do everything well. They can see through all of the "busyness" that level of activity implies, and wonder what, if anything, the student is truly interested in. The mission of the admissions committee is to put together a *freshman class* that is well rounded. That means some serious thinkers, some athletes, some do-gooders, some musicians, some economics majors, and some science majors.

If you believe the myth, you are going to work hard to cram your essay full of evidence of all the wonderful things you do. This method won't succeed for two important reasons. First, the myth is just that, a myth. Admissions directors aren't looking for students who can do it all. Second, you have only got about 500 words. You can't possibly write a great personal essay in that space if you load it up with too much content. Think small. Write about something you are truly interested in or passionate about. Resist the temptation to wow them with too much.

RULE #9: Write a Compelling Introduction

Your introduction must immediately engage admissions officers, enticing them to read further. There are a number of effective ways to hook your reader from the very first sentences of your essay.

● GOOF-PROOF IT! ●

Admissions officers are busy people. They read hundreds of essays at a time. The first person who reads your essay will give it about two or three minutes, before moving on to the next of dozens of other essays ahead of him or her. That means your introduction needs to grab your reader's attention immediately. Unlike other types of writing, the introduction to your college essay should not be a summary, which gives your reader a good excuse to put it down. Why continue reading if they have learned what you are going to say in the first paragraph?

The best way to write a compelling introduction is to *wait to write it until you have completed the rough draft of the rest of your essay.* Then, extract something from your writing to use as an opener.

● GOOF-PROOF CHECKLIST ●

Here are some great ways to create a hook for your reader:

✓ **Get emotional.** Your reader will relate to your subject if you engage their emotions and cause them to make a connection with you and your writing. Think about beginning with the way you felt about something, rather than first describing or otherwise revealing that something.

✓ **Be intriguing.** Your introduction needs to relate to the rest of your essay, but there can be a small detail that makes the admissions officers wonder what you are up to. If you are writing about how your music teacher has influenced you, you might begin by describing him playing his cello in a few detailed sentences. Don't mention yet that he is your teacher, or that he has helped shape your love of music. The reader will wonder who the mystery man is, and want to read on to find out.

✓ **Give an anecdote.** A very short slice of life story that doesn't necessarily clue the reader in to where you are headed can be a great hook. Write about the last seconds of a basketball game, checking out your last customer of the day, your brilliant but disorganized teacher's lecture on Emerson. Admissions officers will have to keep reading to discover what you are writing about.

✓ **Ask a question.** "When have you ever heard of a basketball coach reading poetry to her team?" "Why would I want to give up my poolside summer as a lifeguard to work in a rundown, non-air-conditioned school?" Take your subject and first ask yourself what is unusual or in need of an explanation. Turn it into a question that doesn't have an obvious answer.

✓ **Cite an unusual fact.** Telling your reader something he or she doesn't know, and probably wouldn't guess, can compel him or her to read on. If you are writing about a travel experience, hunt down some statistics that might seem startling. "The U.S. Department of Transportation reported that during the month I was traveling, over 255,000 pieces of luggage were lost." Did your church youth group volunteer with migrant farm workers picking oranges? A few minutes of research can help you begin your essay, "Florida's Valencia orange forecast for April was 86 million boxes."

● GOOF-PROOF EXAMPLE ●
INTRODUCTIONS THAT HOOK THE READER

- I will never forget the moment I landed in Rio de Janeiro, Brazil. As the plane descended, I was awed by the dynamic geography and the juxtaposition of the sea, the mountains, and the city's skyline. I absorbed the landscape further and my eyes focused on the *favelas* mounted on the hillsides.

Why it works: This introduction takes the reader to an exotic location, describing the landscape and setting the scene. He tells you the moment is unforgettable, and brings you along with him. But, more important, he does not reveal anything about his subject. You have to read on to find out what his essay is about.

- My thoughts were scattered. I couldn't concentrate on the directions I was being given, and my anxiety about taking the test only increased as I realized I needed to be paying attention. The more I told myself to relax, the worse it got. Palms sweating, heart beating wildly, I somehow got my gear on and jumped into the pool.

Why it works: Who hasn't felt anxiety before a test? Using emotion as a hook works not only because anyone can relate to those feelings, but also because the reader has no idea what kind of test is being taken. The mention of the pool gives some information without revealing the true subject.

- Tom Wessels slaps his felt hat over his bushy hair, and starts striding away with the confident gait of a hiker. The gritty March snow stings our eyes as we scramble to keep up with him, this master of the woods, wise man of the hills. His book, *Reading the Forested Landscape*, has been our Bible at the Mountain School, an eternal reference to the woods. Few people get to meet the authors of books they read, so we speak to him with special reverence.

Why it works: The reader gets to meet Tom Wessels in a well-written description of both the author and the setting in which the writer meets him. There is no indication where the essay is headed—it could be about Mr. Wessels as an influence, or about his book. In fact, it is really about the writer's love of the natural world, and how it was enhanced by his studies at the Mountain School, and the book *Reading the Forested Landscape*.

RULE #10: Use the Body of Your Essay Effectively

Tell your story seamlessly, using transitions to move from one point to the next.

• GOOF-PROOF IT! •

The body of your essay should be the easiest part to write. Using your outline and notes, write down your thoughts in clear sentences that flow logically from one to another. Remember that you are writing a rough draft; don't sweat every word. If you find weaknesses with your outline as you write, such as missing details or a paragraph that would work better in another part of your essay, make adjustments. There will be plenty of time to refine your essay during the revision and editing processes.

• GOOF-PROOF RULE OF THUMB • MAKING CONNECTIONS

There should be an obvious connection between your introduction and the body of your essay. Don't waste a dynamic start by dumping the reader into a new context that leaves him or her asking, "Where am I?" Show clearly why you began as you did. For example, if you opened with a statistic (such as in Rule #9 about Valencia oranges), the next sentence must connect the numbers with your own experience. It might be, "My youth group had a hard enough time packing a dozen boxes of oranges a day. It's hard to imagine how much work is represented by 86 million boxes."

• GOOF-PROOF EXAMPLE • DON'T FORGET TO USE TRANSITIONS

From sentence to sentence and paragraph to paragraph, use transitions to make your essay flow. As you move from one point to another, develop your ideas logically. The following example shows how transitions pull together an essay that is divided into distinct paragraphs. Note that the author does not rely on over-used transition words and phrases, such as *in addition to, then,* or *since.* It is the repetition of the subjects of soccer and the author's grandmother that relate the paragraphs to one another.

Sunday. As the bus bumps along through the muggy heat of July, I find it hard to be proud. Although I have just played great soccer in the Eastern Regional Tournament and am on my way to Regional Camp to compete with sixty other girls for positions on the East Coast Select Team, I feel tremendously nervous and inferior. Yet when I call my parents that night and learn that my grandmother is in the hospital, I realize that this week of competition is going to be much more challenging emotionally than physically.

Wednesday. I haven't been playing very well; I'm on the reserve team and my chances for advancement are slim. There is only one person who can improve my mood: my mother. Somehow she always knows just what to say. That night I call to tell her about my day and let her cheer me up. Instead, she tells me that my grandmother's situation is worse. The news hits me like a physical blow. My mind starts reeling with thoughts of my grandmother: the way she would pour her coffee into water glasses if it wasn't scalding hot, her soft, all-encompassing bear hugs, her smiling voice over the phone. The thought of this plump, joyful woman I love so much lying in a sterile hospital bed is too painful to think about, so I lose myself in a fantasy novel.

Thursday morning. Now I'm really playing poorly; my mind is on my grandmother, not my soccer ball. I look up across the field—and see my mother walking slowly toward me. I know. She's there to bring me to visit my grandmother, maybe for the last time.

Thursday afternoon. The hospital visit is eerie. My grandmother looks as if she is just barely alive, willing herself to take one more breath. I talk to her about camp, about how good the other players are, and how my game hasn't been my best. She doesn't reply, but I know she hears me. She loves that I play soccer, always telling me how lucky I am to be on a team of girls, and basking in my tales of games won and lost. My mother wants me to stay home and visit the hospital again tomorrow. I'm not sure.

Friday, a little after 11:00 A.M. After much debate, I have decided to return to the Regional Camp for the last game. I know my grandmother wants me to finish what I'd started. I also feel I have an obligation to myself to follow through: I have worked so hard and so long to get to this point that I would be letting myself down if I didn't grasp my last opportunity to be selected. The coaches put me on the advanced team, and I block out all thoughts of my grandmother and play my heart out—for 15 minutes. The game ends. Regional Camp is over, and I haven't made the team. This is the first time someone has told me I'm not good enough at soccer and it hurts.

RULE #11: Finish with a Flourish

When you reach the conclusion, resist the urge to merely summarize the body of your essay.

● GOOF-PROOF IT! ●

End your college essay memorably. Just as with your introduction, you don't want to bore your reader. What kind of final impression will an admissions officer have if he puts down your essay before he's done reading it to the end because of a weak finish?

● GOOF-PROOF CHECKLIST ●

Part 1: Here are three important conclusion blunders to avoid:

- ✓ **Answering the big questions.** If you wrote about a topic such as inner city violence or a personal tragedy, resist the temptation to give reasons or solutions. You don't need to explain why there is discord in the world, or why tragedy is life-affirming.
- ✓ **Using overused words and phrases.** Too many essays end with *therefore, in conclusion,* or *in summary.* End in your own voice, using fresh words and phrases.
- ✓ **Summarizing your essay.** The biggest blunder; the essay is short enough that you can expect your reader to remember what you wrote a few paragraphs ago. Summaries are boring, and waste your opportunity to leave your reader with something memorable.

Part 2: Here are seven ways to echo the dynamic start of your essay.

- ✓ **Continue your discussion.** Propose where it might lead, what it might mean to future generations, or how it might be resolved.

✓ **Make sense of what happened.** If you told a story that would benefit from an explanation of what it means to you in larger terms, take a few sentences to explain. What did you learn? How will you benefit from the experience?

✓ **Connect your content with the desire for a college education.** What does it say about your decision to apply, specifically, to their college?

✓ **Echo your introduction to provide balance.** Use a few of the same words or a phrase from your first paragraph.

✓ **Bring the reader to the present day.** This works especially well if you wrote about something that happened in your past. What does it say about who you are now? How has it influenced the plans you are making for the future?

✓ **End with words on the subject said by someone famous.** Be certain the quote substantiates what you have said, speaks obviously to your topic, and is quoted precisely and accurately.

✓ **Enlarge your discussion by linking it to a wider context.** Your weeklong, hands-on experience with the problems of a small group of migrant farm workers could conclude with a paragraph on the widespread nature of the problem.

● GOOF-PROOF EXAMPLE ●
WINNING CONCLUSIONS

Here is the conclusion to the body essay example found in Rule #10. It concludes by making sense of what happened:

Friday afternoon. I am on my way home, staring out the car window, seeing, yet not seeing, the trees rush by. As I reflect back on the past few days, I realize that I have grown. There is a strength within me that held firm through a pair of difficult events that came to me simultaneously. I can call on that strength when I need it in the future, as I continue to strive for success.

In the conclusion to the essay introduction found in Rule #9 the writer continues his discussion by expanding the lesson about familiar landscapes to encompass those that are unfamiliar or as yet unmade.

Wessels has not only permitted me to read his book at home, to constantly observe and note details of familiar woods to give me a story, but he has also allowed me to question the lands I've never been to before, and let me imagine and speculate vast forests of the future, places that have never been, and may never be, save for the realm of imagination.

RULE #12: Watch What You Read

What you read can influence what you write.

● GOOF-PROOF IT! ●

From the beginning of your essay writing process, you should be aware of what you are reading. The old computer science term "garbage in, garbage out" applies: If you are reading a steady diet of mediocre writing, you are missing a great opportunity to improve your own writing. Syntax and style can improve when you add some great writing to your print diet.

This trick is too simple to not follow. Once you get in the habit, consider keeping it—the point is not that you will copy the good writing you read, but that it will be a positive influence. Your style, structure, and even vocabulary can improve when you are exposed to high quality writing. Therefore, if your literary diet consists of enticing yet averagely written novels or flashy entertainment magazines, put them aside for a while and pick up something new.

What should you read? We have polled English professors and teachers, college counselors and admissions officers for their ideas. Here is a list of books and periodicals that offer pieces on current events, book reviews, science, history, race relations, sports, and other topics. Choose essays that appeal to you; there is no need to force yourself to read about something that holds little personal interest. You can be assured of finding superior writing on a wide variety of subjects in the following:

- *The Atlantic* (monthly): reporting and commentary on contemporary issues, fiction, and columns on travel and food.
- *The Economist* (weekly): London publication covering world news, finance and economics, science and technology, books and arts, and business news.
- *Harper's* (monthly): essays; fiction; and reporting on political, literary, cultural, and scientific affairs.

- *The New Yorker* (weekly): political and business reporting, social commentary, fiction, humor, art, poetry, and criticism.
- Atwan, Robert and Stephen J. Gould, eds. *Best American Essays 2002* (Boston: Houghton Mifflin, 2002): annual publication—any year is fine; all volumes include a wide range of subjects.
- DiYanni, Robert. *One Hundred Great Essays* (New York: Longman, 2001): great variety, including works by Queen Elizabeth I, Benjamin Franklin, Zora Neale Hurston, James Thurber, and Amy Tan.
- American Society of Magazine Editors. *The Best American Magazine Writing of 2002* (New York: Harper, 2002): includes pieces on science, sports, current events, personalities, and fiction.

● PUTTING IT ALL TOGETHER ●

Spend time on your rough draft. Organize your essay so it moves logically from paragraph to paragraph, and understand your audience and what they are looking for. Use each part of the essay, introduction, body, and conclusion effectively, and avoid common errors that can weaken your writing.

● GOOF-PROOF GUIDELINES ●

- Create an outline for your essay by indicating major and minor points, details, and examples.
- Check your outline to see that your essay flows from one point to the next in a logical way. Be certain you have enough supporting details to make your essay fresh and vital.
- Use many types of details to help the reader to connect with your writing. They make your writing uniquely your own and add vital interest. The addition of details can turn a weak essay into a winner.

- Your essay is also referred to as a *personal statement*. It is not your writing skills or intellectual prowess that will wow the admissions committee. What they are looking for in the essay is the *personal* or emotional connection they can make with you.
- Admissions officers are assigned hundreds of essays to read, and can spend just a few minutes on each one. Engage them immediately so they are interested enough to keep reading.
- Wait to write your introduction until after you have completed a rough draft of the body of your essay.
- Use your outline and notes as a guide for writing the body, putting down your thoughts in clear sentences that flow logically from one to another. You have plenty of time to refine your rough draft later, so don't obsess over every word.
- When you reach the conclusion, resist the urge to summarize the body of your essay. There are more effective ways to leave your reader with a memorable impression.
- Since what you read has an influence on what you write, use your leisure time reading to improve the quality of your writing. Choose books, newspapers, and periodicals that offer fine examples of essays and journalism. Your vocabulary and writing style will get a boost.

THE GOOF – UP:
WRITING WITHOUT CLARITY

College admissions staff must read thousands of essays, and can only afford to spend a few minutes on each one. Therefore you not only want to impress them with your unique take on a topic, you need to say exactly what you mean as clearly and as quickly as possible.

Remember that your goal is to convey information about yourself. That goal won't be achieved if your readers don't understand your first few sentences or paragraphs and stop reading, or if they finish reading but fail to grasp your message. Learning how to be a clear and accurate writer will help make your essay not only more readable, but also will guarantee that those who read it understand exactly what you mean to say.

RULE #13: Make Modifiers Work for You

Well-chosen, specific adjectives and adverbs make your point clear, adding meaning as well as originality to your writing.

● GOOF-PROOF IT! ●

Word choice is important when trying to make a point clearly. In Section Two, you learned to use details to add clarity and originality. Powerful adverbs and adjectives (modifiers) perform a similar function: They can convey your ideas with greater style and more shades of meaning.

● GOOF-PROOF EXAMPLE ● MAKE IT STAND OUT

Tom put his hat on, and walked away.

Tom Wessels slaps his felt hat over his bushy hair, and starts striding away with the confident gait of a mountain trekker.

Consider the difference between these two sentences. The latter example allows you to hear the voice and impressions of the writer, providing a more accurate and interesting picture of the action. The first sentence is simply dull.

While this example demonstrates how details improve your writing, there are instances when the right modifiers can get your message across in fewer, more accurate words. This is critical in a personal statement that is limited to two pages or 500 words. You don't want to sacrifice unique details, but sometimes one word will do the job better than three or four. For example, *promptly* can take the place of *in a few days*; *productive* can take the place of *much was accomplished*.

● GOOF-PROOF EXAMPLE ●
SOME POWERFUL, PRECISE
ADJECTIVES AND ADVERBS

- directly involved
- unflagging dedication
- promptly accepted
- productive discussion
- grueling game
- instinctively aware
- influential teacher
- invaluable learning experience

RULE #14: Be Concise

Most schools require you to limit your personal statement to 500 words, or two pages. That means you can't waste words. Learn the most common, unnecessary "word wasters" so you can avoid them when writing your essay.

● GOOF-PROOF IT! ●

You learned in Rule #13 that you can eliminate unnecessary words and phrases by using well-chosen modifiers. In addition, there are a number of well-known (and overused) words and phrases that should be eliminated from your writing because they aren't necessary, or should be altered to a shorter form. These are the four worst offenders, followed by examples.

1. *Because of the fact that.* In most cases, just *because* will do.

   Because of the fact that it rained, the game was canceled.
   Because it rained, the game was canceled.

2. *That* and *which* phrases. Eliminate them by turning the idea in the *that* or *which* phrase into an adjective.

   This was a course that was very helpful.
   This course was very helpful.

   The game, which lasted three hours, ended at nine.
   The three-hour game ended at nine.

3. *There is, it is.* These constructions avoid the direct approach and are often unnecessary. Instead, use a clear agent of action:

   It was with regret that I left the school for the last time.
   I left the school for the last time with regret.

   There is no reason I can find to make another choice.
   I can find no reason to make another choice.

4. *That* by itself is a word that often clutters sentences unnecessarily, as in the following example:

> He said that he thought that my contribution was useful and that he was happy that there will be more opportunities for me to get involved.
>
> He said he thought my contribution was useful, and he was happy there will be more opportunities for me to get involved.

● GOOF-PROOF EXAMPLE ●
WORD CHOICES FOR CONCISE WRITING

WORDY:	REPLACE WITH:
a lot of	*many* or *much*
all of a sudden	*suddenly*
along the lines of	*like*
are able to	*can*
as a matter of fact	*in fact* or Delete
as a person	Delete
as a whole	Delete
as the case may be	Delete
at the present time	*currently* or *now*
basic necessity	*necessity*
both of these	*both*
by and large	Delete
by definition	Delete
compare and contrast	*compare*
due to the fact that	*because*
final destination	*destination*
for all intents and purposes	Delete
has a tendency to	*often* or Delete
has the ability to	*can*
in order to	*to*
in the event that	*if*
in the near future	*soon*
is able to	*can*
it is clear that	Delete

last but not least	*finally*
on a daily basis	*daily*
on account of the fact that	*because*
particular	Delete
period of time	*period* or *time*
somewhere in the neighborhood of	*about*
take action	*act*
the fact that	*that* or Delete
the majority of	*most*
the reason why	*the reason* or *why*
through the use of	*through*
totally obvious	*obvious*
with regard to	*about* or *regarding*
with the exception of	*except for*

● GOOF-PROOF EXAMPLE ●
WORDY AND CONCISE SENTENCES

Wordy: The students who were late missed the first set of awards.

Concise: The late students missed the first set of awards.

Wordy: It is my feeling that the problem of global warming should be addressed immediately.

Concise: I feel the global warming problem should be addressed immediately.

Wordy: I think that there is the possibility that the guidance counselor who was recently hired is a graduate of your college.

Concise: I think the new guidance counselor may be a graduate of your college.

RULE #15: Eliminate Ambiguity

Don't confuse your readers by using the wrong words, or by using the right words in the wrong order.

● **GOOF-PROOF IT!** ●

Ambiguous means having two or more possible meanings. The problem with ambiguous language is that the meaning understood by the reader may not be the one intended by the writer. There are two important guidelines to follow to avoid ambiguity:

1. Refrain from using words and phrases with more than one meaning.
2. Be sure the words you use are in the right order to convey your intended meaning.

● **GOOF-PROOF EXAMPLE** ●
MAKE IT CLEAR

During my photojournalism class, I snapped away at the model.

This sentence can be read two ways: you *snapped* pictures with a camera, or you verbally snapped at the model because you were agitated. This kind of confusion can happen whenever a word has more than one possible meaning. *During my photojournalism class, I took pictures of the model* is a better sentence.

My customer ate the sandwich with the blue hat.

Here, the *word order* of the sentence, not an individual word, causes the confusion. Did the customer eat her sandwich with her hat? Because the phrase *with the blue hat* is in the wrong place, the meaning of the sentence is unclear. Try instead: *My customer with the blue hat ate the sandwich.*

● GOOF-PROOF EXAMPLE ●
CORRECTING AMBIGUOUS LANGUAGE

Ambiguous: When reaching for the phone, the coffee spilled on the table.

Clear: The coffee spilled on the table when you reached for the phone.

Ambiguous: I went to see the doctor with a severe headache.

Clear: I went to see the doctor because I had a severe headache.

Ambiguous: The famous artist drew stares when he entered the room.

Clear: The famous artist received stares when he entered the room.

Ambiguous: When writing on the computer, the spell checker often comes in handy.

Clear: The spell checker often comes in handy when I am writing on the computer.

RULE #16: Avoid Unclear Pronoun References

Pronouns should be used only when it is certain to whom they refer.

• GOOF-PROOF IT! •

Another common mistake that interferes with clarity is the use of unclear pronoun references. Pronouns, such as *me, you, he,* and *she,* replace nouns. Consider these two cases:

I went to school every day with Ted and Fred, and we took his car.

Whose car? *His* could mean either Ted's or Fred's. The writer needs to use a proper name instead of the pronoun in order to eliminate the possibility the reader will not understand him or her. Write instead: *Ted picked Fred and me up for school each morning, so we could all go together.*

They considered publishing our poems in the anthology.

This is a common pronoun error: using a vague *they* when there are specific people behind an action, but the writer does not know exactly who those people are. Even without that information, you can revise it to be more precise: *The publishing company considered publishing our poems in their anthology.*

• GOOF-PROOF EXAMPLE •
UNCLEAR PRONOUN REFERENCES, WITH CORRECTIONS

Vague: *They* passed new environmental legislation yesterday.
Clear: *The State Senate* passed new environmental legislation yesterday.

Vague: Mr. Jones told James that he had found *his* missing report.
Clear: Mr. Jones told James that he had found *James's* missing report.

Vague: *They* closed the movie theater after they discovered several fire code violations.

Clear: *The owners* of the movie theater closed their doors after they discovered several fire code violations.

Vague: The police officer arrested the man after *he* joined the protestors.

Clear: After the man joined the protestors, *he* was arrested by a police officer.

RULE #17: Avoid Unnecessary Repetition

Saying the same idea more than once wastes your reader's time.
Get it right the first time, and move on.

● **GOOF-PROOF IT!** ●

Another way to lose your reader, or simply waste time, is to state an idea or piece of information more than once. Writers repeat themselves unnecessarily because they are not sure that they have been clear, or they are not attentive to the need to be concise. Repetition in your personal statement can take two forms: word choice and content.

Word choice refers to the use of unnecessary words and phrases that simply repeat information already given.

Consider these cases:

Repetitive: The awards ceremony was held at 4:00 P.M. in the afternoon.
Concise: The awards ceremony was held at 4:00 P.M.

P.M. means in the afternoon, so there's no reason to say *in the afternoon.* It's a waste of words and the reader's time.

Repetitive: As I pointed out in my list of extra-curricular activities, I was elected to student council four years in a row and spent two years as president.
Concise: I was elected to student council four years in a row, and I spent two years as president.

Content refers to the personal information you are writing about. The essay is not the place to repeat information that can be found elsewhere on the application. For instance, you have already listed your extra-curricular activities and GPA that have been noted by the admissions committee; there is no need to remind them of these accomplishments. Use your essay to tell your readers something they don't know about you.

Keep the content of your essay fresh and inventive, telling your readers something they couldn't have learned from the rest of your application. Then, be certain your word choices aren't repetitive. Goof-Proof it by saying it quickly and clearly the first time.

● GOOF-PROOF EXAMPLE ●
REPETITIVE SENTENCES

Wordy: The room is red in color.
Concise: The room is red.

Wordy: It was essential that everyone arrived promptly and on time.
Concise: It was essential that everyone arrived on time.

Wordy: It's time to terminate the project and put an end to it.
Concise: It's time to terminate the project.

Wordy: The car that is gray in color must have been in an accident or collision.
Concise: The gray car must have been in an accident.

Wordy: Please let me know your plans as soon as possible and at your earliest convenience.
Concise: Please let me know your plans as soon as possible.

Wordy: I had to think carefully before revealing my wish list and desires.
Concise: I had to think carefully before revealing my wish list.

RULE #18: Think Twice before Opening Your Thesaurus

Big words won't win points with your readers. Aim to sound like yourself, not to impress with your knowledge of ten-letter words.

● GOOF-PROOF IT! ●

Admissions directors and college counselors give this piece of advice often: Don't use words specifically to show off your vocabulary or to try to wow your reader. There is an important difference between using just the right word to convey meaning and using a bigger, longer word when a simpler one will do.

Not convinced to put down your thesaurus? Here are three reasons to stop looking for and using so-called big words.

1. **They sound pretentious.** Remember, you are supposed to sound like you, not a politician or chairman-of-the-board.
2. **They can sound ridiculous.** By using words that are not in your normal vocabulary, you run the risk of using them incorrectly.
3. **They may appear as a tactic.** Your reader might think you are trying to add weight with words because you are worried your essay isn't well written or that your ideas aren't worth reading.

● GOOF-PROOF EXAMPLE ● USE YOUR OWN VOICE

To the point: I decided to keep it simple by packing only those things that I could carry in one suitcase.

Thesaurized: I determined to eschew obfuscation by packing only those things that I could transport in one valise.

To the point:　In high school I took my first accounting class and began to help my mother with the accounting tasks of the business.

Thesaurized:　In secondary school I took my first accounting class and commenced to aid my mother with the accounting functions of the business.

To the point:　At my summer job, I had the chance to learn about Information Technology as it relates to engineering.

Thesaurized:　At my summer employment, I had the fortuity to obtain IT-related information as it pertains to the engineering field.

● PUTTING IT ALL TOGETHER ●

Admissions essay writing is about conveying information about yourself in a way that gets a positive reaction from your reader. If that information doesn't make sense, gets lost in poor writing, or bores your audience, you have not succeeded. Learn how to say what you mean clearly and quickly so your essay brings you one step closer to acceptance at the school(s) of your choice.

● GOOF-PROOF GUIDELINES ●

- Well-chosen, specific modifiers (adjectives and adverbs) clarify meaning and bring originality to your writing.
- Keep in mind that your essay will be read in just a couple of minutes by someone who has hundreds of other essays to read as well. Admissions officers are busy people and can't be bothered trying to figure out what you mean.
- Don't use many words when a few will do, and don't waste time by repeating yourself.
- Avoid ambiguous language: Don't use words whose multiple meanings may cause confusion; be certain the order of words in your sentences conveys the meaning you intend.
- Check your pronouns: Is it absolutely clear to whom or what they refer?
- Bigger words are not better: Don't use your thesaurus to replace simple, direct language.

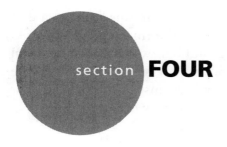

THE GOOF – UP:
CHOOSING THE WRONG WORDS

One of the best ways to accurately convey your ideas in your essay is to choose the right words. Doing so ensures that your audience understands the meaning you intend.

This sounds simple, and for the most part, it is. You already have a command of the English language that includes knowledge of thousands of words' *denotative* (literal, primary) meanings. Therefore, all you need to do is choose the right ones to get your message across.

Saying what you mean, however, takes more than just an understanding of the denotative meaning of a word. Many words have not just a denotative meaning, but also a *connotative* meaning. The connotation is a word's implied meaning, which involves emotions, cultural assumptions, and suggestions. Both meanings must be considered when making word choices.

Once you are certain of denotative and connotative meaning, you must consider whether the words you choose might confuse or put off the admissions committee. That means being aware of inclusive language, the proper level of formality, and overused language (such as clichés, slang, and buzzwords). Your personal statement is an important opportunity to get a positive message across. Don't miss it by inadvertently insulting, confusing, or annoying your reader by using the wrong word(s).

RULE #19: Learn the Most Commonly Confused Words, and Use Them Properly

Commonly confused words sound or look similar, but have different meanings.

• GOOF-PROOF IT! •

Pay attention to the meaning of every word that you use. If you are unsure that the word you have chosen is correct, look it up in your dictionary (or refer to the list of commonly confused words below). When you misuse words, your writing suffers. One wrong word—using *illicit* when you mean *elicit,* for example—can completely change the meaning of an otherwise well-written essay. It can also result in making your reader question your intelligence.

The following list contains 20 of the most commonly confused word pairs or groups, along with a brief definition of each. Check your essay for them, making sure you have used the correct word. You might want to make flash cards for each pair or group, and use the cards to learn the definitions so your future writing improves as well.

• GOOF-PROOF EXAMPLE •
COMMONLY CONFUSED WORDS CLARIFIED

CONFUSING WORDS	QUICK DEFINITION
accept	recognize
except	excluding
access	means of approaching
excess	extra
affect	to influence
effect (noun)	result
effect (verb)	to bring about

assure	to make certain (assure someone)
ensure	to make certain
insure	to make certain (financial value)
beside	next to
besides	in addition to
bibliography	list of references
biography	a life story
complement	match
compliment	praise
decent	well-mannered
descent	decline, fall
desert	arid, sandy region
dessert	sweet served after a meal
disburse	to pay
disperse	to spread out
disinterested	no strong opinion either way
uninterested	don't care
elicit	to stir up
illicit	illegal
farther	beyond
further	additional
imply	hint, suggest
infer	assume, deduce
personal	individual
personnel	employees

principal (adjective)	main
principal (noun)	person in charge
principle	standard
than	in contrast to
then	next
their	belonging to them
there	in a place
they're	they are
who	substitute for he, she, or they
whom	substitute for him, her, or them
your	belonging to you
you're	you are

[QUIZ #1]

Do you know the difference between these confusing word pairs?
Choose the correct word to complete each sentence. The answers
can be found in Appendix B on page 173.

1. I (assured / ensured) my parents that I was making the right decision.
2. (There / Their) game was held last Saturday.
3. We enjoyed our trip to Boston better (then / than)
   our trip to Phoenix.
4. The (personal / personnel) office is in the back
   of the building.
5. To (who / whom) should I address this letter?

RULE #20: Learn the Most Misused Words, and Use Them Properly

There are a number of words that are misused frequently. Learn them so you will use them correctly.

● GOOF-PROOF IT! ●

Choosing the right words also means being aware of the many commonly misused ones. You may find examples of misused words every day in the media, on billboards and other signs, in speech, and in writing. In fact, even when used incorrectly, these words often sound acceptable to many writers. But they will stand out to admissions officers as glaring errors. Take the time to learn their denotative meanings, and avoid an embarrassing mistake.

● GOOF-PROOF EXAMPLE ●
DIFFERENTIATING FREQUENTLY MISUSED WORDS

WORD	WHEN TO USE IT
Amount	used when you cannot count the items to which you are referring, and when referring to singular nouns
Number	used when you can count the items to which you are referring, and when referring to plural nouns
Anxious	nervous
Eager	enthusiastic, or looking forward to something
Among	used when comparing or referring to three or more people or things
Between	used for two people or things
Bring	moving something toward the speaker
Take	moving something away from the speaker

Goof-Proof Hint: Remember, bring to, take away.

Can:	used to state ability
May:	used to state permission

Each other:	when referring to two people or things
One another:	when referring to three or more people or things

e.g.:	an abbreviation for the Latin "exempli gratia," meaning *free example* or *for example*
i.e.:	an abbreviation for the Latin "id est," meaning *it is* or *that is*

Feel bad:	used when talking about emotional feelings
Feel badly:	used when talking about physically feeling something

Fewer:	when you can count the items
Less:	when you cannot count the items

Good:	an adjective, which describes a person, place, or thing
Well:	an adverb, which describes an action or verb

Its:	belonging to *it*
It's:	contraction of *it is*

Goof-Proof Hint: Unlike most possessives, it doesn't have an apostrophe.

Lay:	the action of placing or putting an item somewhere; a transitive verb, meaning something you do *to* something else
Lie:	to recline or be placed (a lack of action); an intransitive verb, meaning it does not act on anything or anyone else

More:	used to compare one thing to another
Most:	used to compare one thing to more than one other thing

That: a pronoun that introduces a restrictive (or essential) clause

Which: a pronoun that introduces a non-restrictive (or unessential) clause

Goof-Proof Hint: Imagine a parenthetical *by the way* following the word *which*. "The book, which (by the way) Jo prefers, is her first novel," is incorrect. Therefore, it should read "The book that Jo prefers is her first novel." "Lou's pants, which (by the way) are black, are made of leather," is correct.

QUIZ #2

Answer the following to test your knowledge of commonly mis-used words. The answers can be found in Appendix B on pages 173–174.

1. My brother was being indecisive, so I was forced to decide (among / between) the two movies.
2. After working long hours for three months, Joan was (eager / anxious) to start her vacation.
3. I lost the game but didn't (feel bad / feel badly) because I'd tried my best.
4. Exhausted, she went to her bedroom to (lay / lie) down.
5. The dinner (that / which) we ate last night was delicious.

RULE #21: Don't Use Words That Aren't Really Words

It doesn't matter how often they are used, the words mentioned in this rule are not considered standard English and should never be used.

● GOOF-PROOF IT! ●

This rule is the easiest one to follow. Learn the following list and always avoid these words in your writing.

● GOOF-PROOF EXAMPLE ●
DROP THESE WORDS FROM YOUR VOCABULARY

acrossed/acrost	the adverb and preposition *across* has only one form; it never ends in the letter *t*
alot	incorrect spelling of *a lot;* often seen in informal writing, but should not be used in the essay or any other formal writing
anyways	speech dialect form not acceptable in written English; use *anyway*
anywheres	speech dialect form not acceptable in written English; use *anywhere*
brang/brung	often seen masquerading as the past tense of *bring; brought* is the only correct past tense of bring
everywheres	speech dialect form not acceptable in written English; use *everywhere*
hopefully	most often heard as a substitute for "I hope;" as such it is not a word. "*Hopefully* I'll get an A of the test" is an example of non-standard English. What the writer means is "I hope I'll get an A on the test." *Hopefully* is a word, however, when used as an adverb to mean

	full of hope. For example: They waited *hopefully* for the firefighters.
irregardless	this blend of irrespective and regardless has been in use for about a century, but is still not considered a word in standard written English
majorly/minorly	major and minor are adjectives; these substandard forms are attempts to use the words as adverbs. Other words, such as "somewhat," should be used instead.
nowheres	speech dialect form not acceptable in written English; use *nowhere*
somewheres	speech dialect form not acceptable in written English; use *somewhere*
theirselves/themself	both are incorrect forms of *themselves;* because *them* is plural, *self* must be as well. Also, *their* combined with *selves* is incorrect because it suggests possession.

QUIZ #3

Rewrite the following sentences in standard English. The answers can be found in Appendix B on page 174.

1. He brang a calculator with him to the calculus final.
2. Hopefully the meeting will go well.
3. Anywheres you want to meet for lunch is fine with me.
4. Irregardless of the weather, we are going to play golf.
5. People should take responsibility for themself.

RULE #22: Don't Use Words or Phrases That Might Offend Your Reader

Whether or not its use is intentional, biased language can inflict harm on others. Always avoid bias in your writing.

● GOOF-PROOF IT! ●

It is imperative that your writing is free of biased language, including the use of negative stereotypes, which may result in the exclusion or putting down of others. Your goal is to include rather than to exclude. Understanding the purpose of inclusive language and using it in your essay, will ensure that your message gets across as intended, without causing offense. Replace any possibly offensive words and phrases with inclusive language that doesn't offend or degrade another person.

● GOOF-PROOF CHECKLIST ●

Here are types of bias to avoid in your writing:

Gender
✓ Avoid the suffix *-ess,* which has the effect of minimizing the significance of the word to which it is attached (*actor* is preferable to *actress, proprietor* to *proprietress*).
✓ Do not overuse *he* and *him*. Instead, use *his or her* or, if plural, *their* and *those;* or alternate between *him* and *her*.
✓ Degender titles. *Businessman* becomes *businessperson* or *executive, chairman* becomes *chair* or *chairperson, stewardess* becomes *flight attendant, weatherman* becomes *meteorologist*.
✓ When referring to a couple, don't make any assumptions. *Inappropriate:* Mr. Rosenberg and Caryn, Mr. and Mrs. Bill Rosenberg. *Appropriate:* Mr. Rosenberg and Ms. Fetzer.

✓ Use professional, rather than personal, descriptive terms. *Inappropriate:* Robin Benoit, a lovely novelist. *Appropriate:* Robin Benoit, an experienced novelist.

Race
✓ To avoid stereotyping, leave out any reference to race, unless it is relevant to the subject of your writing.
✓ Focus on a person's individual, professional characteristics and qualifications, not racial characteristics.

Disability
✓ Discuss the *person,* not their handicap.
✓ If your writing is specifically focused on disabilities or disease, or you must mention them for another reason, don't use words that imply victimization or create negative stereotypes. Terms such as *victim, sufferer, poor, afflicted,* and *unfortunate* should be omitted.
✓ Don't use courageous *to describe a person with a disability unless the context allows the adjective to be used for all. Someone is not courageous because they are deaf, but they may be because they swam the English Channel.*
✓ Always put the person ahead of the disability, as in *person with impaired hearing,* rather than *hearing-impaired person.*

[*QUIZ #4*]

Remove any biased language from the following sentences, and replace it with inclusive words or phrases. If the sentence is appropriate, mark it so. The answers can be found in Appendix B on page 174.

1. The chairman of our committee read a report regarding absenteeism among the waitresses.
2. Every student must put personal belongings in his or her own locker.
3. The African-American tennis players Venus and Serena Williams are the best in the world.

4. Please support the efforts of our brave Vice Principal, Dora Sinclair, by sponsoring her in the Relay for Life.
5. Did you send the invitation to Dr. Choe and Tannie?

RULE #23: Understand Positive and Negative Connotations to Choose Words Wisely

Connotative, or implied, meanings can be positive, negative, or neutral. Using a word without being aware of its implied meaning can offend your reader or make your message unclear.

● GOOF-PROOF IT! ●

Connotation involves emotions, cultural assumptions, and suggestions. Some dictionaries offer usage notes that help to explain connotative meanings, but they alone can't be relied on when trying to avoid offensive or incorrect word choices.

For example, what feelings come to mind when you hear the word *skinny? Thin? Skinny* has negative connotations, while *thin* is a more neutral selection. *Copy* or *plagiarize? Leer* or *look?*

If you were writing about a bonding exercise during which your teachers played favorite childhood games, you wouldn't choose the adjective *childish* to describe their behavior. *Childish* has a connotative meaning of immaturity, whereas *childlike,* a better choice, does not.

Similarly, the words *vagrant* and *homeless* have the same denotative meaning. However, *vagrant* connotes a public nuisance, whereas *homeless* suggests an unfortunate situation worthy of attention and assistance.

Imagine that you are writing about a friend's unfortunate experience with law enforcement. This episode was extremely embarrassing, and you want to minimize its importance. You wouldn't say he was *busted.* This word has a connotative meaning of a violent overtaking of a criminal by the police. The term *arrest* is more neutral, whereas *police detention* sounds as positive as you can be with regard to a bad situation.

[*QUIZ #5*]

Do the following words have a positive or negative connotation?
The answers can be found in Appendix B on pages 174–175.

1. inexpensive   positive / negative
2. encourage   positive / negative
3. aromatic   positive / negative
4. ludicrous   positive / negative
5. cozy   positive / negative

RULE #24: Formality versus Informality

Your personal statement should strike a balance between formality and informality. You don't want to sound distant and stiff, but a highly informal tone using slang also is inappropriate.

• GOOF-PROOF IT! •

It is crucial that your essay sound like you, not a college professor or a rap artist. Your voice should be another piece of personal information you share with the admissions committee. Let your reader hear *you,* not your impressive vocabulary or your attempt to sound like what you think they want to hear.

The balance you need to strike between formality and informality is simply the avoidance of one extreme or another. You are not writing to your best friend, nor are you writing an academic essay for a scholarly journal. Go back to the journal entries you wrote in Section One. These are written in the voice you want to use, with just the right level of formality.

• GOOF-PROOF CHECKLIST •

Follow these guidelines to ensure that your tone is correct and that you have struck the appropriate level of formality.

- ✓ Avoid slang words and phrases unless you are deliberately trying to imitate speech.
- ✓ A few contractions (*I'm, don't, shouldn't*) can help your essay from sounding too stiff.
- ✓ Aim to sound like yourself, a high school senior.
- ✓ Don't use five words when one will get the point across, or use words considered archaic or pretentious (*according to,* not *as per; determine,* not *ascertain; think about,* not *cogitate*).

✓ If you are worried your writing is too stiff, rewrite a few paragraphs as a mock journal entry, then compare them to your essay. What words or phrases need toning down?

QUIZ #6

Rate the following words as either formal (F), or informal (I). The answers can be found in Appendix B on page 175.

_____ permit
_____ allow

_____ eliminate
_____ get rid of

_____ more
_____ additional

_____ cannot
_____ unable to

_____ help
_____ assist

RULE #25: Avoid Overly Informal and Overused Language

Any form of slang, clichés, specialized, or overused language does not belong in your essay.

• GOOF-PROOF IT! •

Colloquialisms are words and phrases appropriate for speech, and very informal or casual writing. They don't belong in your personal statement unless you are trying to imitate speech or assume a very informal tone for effect. Colloquialisms include vulgarisms (obscene or offensive words), clichés, and slang.

Your reader is not going to consult a dictionary to understand what you have written, nor will he or she be impressed with stale, highly unoriginal language. Eliminate any words or phrases that are overused, or that might be unfamiliar to an admissions officer. A word or two in a foreign language, which you translate immediately, is permissible. The use of confusing technical language or buzzwords is not.

• GOOF-PROOF CHECKLIST •

Here are the usage mistakes to avoid in your essay.

✔ **Vulgarisms.** The last thing you want to do is turn off or offend your reader. Since you do not know your audience, you do not know exactly what kinds of language they may find offensive or in poor taste. Err on the side of caution by not including any language considered even mildly obscene, gross, or otherwise offensive. This includes scatological and sexual terms, and words such as hell (as in "hotter than hell"), God (as in "oh, God!"), and damn.

✔ **Clichés.** Avoid these not only because they are too informal, but also because they are overused. Your writing must be in your own voice, without relying on stale phrases such as: *no* *news is good news; don't worry, be happy; when life gives you lemons, make lemonade;* and *no guts, no glory.*

✓ **Slang.** Slang is non-standard English. Its significance is typically far-removed from either a word's denotative or connotative meaning, and is particular to certain groups (therefore, it excludes some readers who won't understand it). Examples include: *blow off, canned, no sweat,* and *thumbs down (or up).* It is also inappropriate, and in poor taste, to use slang terms for racial or religious groups.

✓ **Buzzwords.** This is really a type of slang that uses big words (real or made up) when simpler words would work better. They are at best pompous, and at worst, confusing. And, like other forms of slang, buzzwords don't belong in your essay. See Rule #18 in Section Three for reasons to put away your thesaurus and otherwise tone down any overzealous impulses to use big words. Examples include: *resultful* (gets results), *suboptimal* (not the best), *guesstimate* (estimate), *requisite* (necessary), *potentiality* (potential), and *facilitate* (help).

✓ **Technobabble.** This type of language could be a problem if you are writing about your involvement with computers or other forms of technology. While it is perfectly acceptable to use the constantly generated new words and highly technical language associated with technology with those whose knowledge of the field is similar to yours, they don't belong in your essay. Your aim is not to confuse your reader, but to enlighten. Don't assume that your audience shares your interests or familiarity with technology; write instead for a reader who has a broad knowledge base that is not expert in any subject. That means explaining anything your reader might not be familiar with, without talking down to him or her.

● GOOF-PROOF EXAMPLE ●
TO BE AVOIDED

24/7 (all the time)
screenagers (teens who are online)
axed (instead of asked)
mouse potato (technology's answer to the couch potato)
my bad (my fault)

● PUTTING IT ALL TOGETHER ●

When writing your essay, you must choose your words carefully. That means understanding their meanings and being sensitive to their power. The wrong words not only make you seem less intelligent, but they can also confuse, annoy, or even offend your reader.

● GOOF-PROOF GUIDELINES ●

- Learn the meanings of commonly confused words (those that sound or look similar, but have different meanings) and end the confusion in your writing.
- Learn the meanings of frequently misused words, and use them correctly.
- Don't use words considered non- or sub-standard English.
- Replace biased language with inclusive language to keep your writing from alienating or offending your audience.
- Understand the positive and negative connotations of the words you use. The wrong connotation can not only confuse, but also offend your readers.
- Strike a balance between formality and informality, and aim to sound like yourself.
- Keep colloquialisms, such as slang and clichés, out of your essay.
- Don't use pompous or confusing jargon, such as techno-babble and buzzwords.

THE GOOF-UP:
MISUNDERSTANDING THE BASIC MECHANICS OF WRITING

No matter how original an idea you come up with, the inability to express yourself clearly and accurately through the written word will hinder the success of your personal statement. The rules of mechanics are complex; in fact, they sometimes confuse even professional writers. However, you do not need to become a strict grammarian in order to write well.

A few dozen grammar, spelling, punctuation, and capitalization mistakes account for the majority of common writing errors. Once you become acquainted with these common errors and learn how to avoid or correct them, your writing will greatly improve. Therefore, this section on mechanics will focus on the errors that occur most frequently.

Your personal statement must show the admissions department that you are someone they want to accept. Every advantage should be used to achieve this goal, including the use of proper spelling, punctuation, and grammar. The following rules will teach you the mechanics of writing you need to know to write a great essay.

RULE #26: Avoid Common Usage Errors with Parts of Speech

Four of the eight major parts of speech represent the majority of usage difficulties. Learning these common errors will help you avoid them and instead write more clear, concise sentences.

● GOOF-PROOF IT! ●

Some parts of speech are more difficult than others. The four most challenging ones as they pertain to your essay are: pronouns, adjectives, adverbs, and prepositions. They will be clarified here, along with usage explanations and examples. If you feel your writing would benefit from a more in-depth review of grammar, go to Appendix A for websites and print resources that contain grammar lessons, practice exercises, and quizzes to reinforce the basics.

● Pronouns

Pronouns refer back to or take the place of nouns. They should:

1. Agree in number (a singular pronoun must be used for a singular noun).

   Incorrect: If *the student* passes this course, *they* will graduate.
   Correct: If *the student* passes this course, *she* will graduate.

2. Agree in person.
   Don't switch back and forth in your writing from the first person (*I*) to the second (*you*) or third (*he, she, they, it*).
   First person pronouns: *I, me, we, us*
   Second person pronoun: *you*
   Third person pronoun: *he, she, him, her, they, them*

3. Be a specific reference to a noun. It should be obvious to your reader which noun the pronoun refers to.

● GOOF-PROOF EXAMPLE ●
PRONOUN AGREEMENT

Incorrect: When *a person* comes to class, *you* should have your homework ready.

Correct: When *a person* comes to class, *he* should have his homework ready.

Incorrect: Tim spends all his time reading and playing soccer, but it isn't
good for him.
—What isn't good for him? Reading, playing soccer, or
  both?

Correct: Tim spends all his time reading and playing soccer. *Too much
soccer* isn't good for him; he should play some basketball,
too.

Incorrect: It's been years since *they* spent money on new textbooks.
—Who are they?

Correct: It's been years since *the school board* spent money on new
textbooks.

Incorrect: I went on the trip with Emily and Nancy, and we took her
laptop.
—Whose laptop?

Correct: I went on the trip with Emily and Nancy, and we took
Nancy's laptop.

● Adjectives

Adjectives describe or modify nouns or pronouns. They add
information by describing people, places, or things in a sentence.
These words, more than any others, make your essay a unique
piece. You can use them to describe people, objects, and situations to make the reader understand your point of view and see
things the way you have seen them. Too few adjectives will make
a personal statement a boring play-by-play that doesn't tell the
reader anything about the writer.

• Adverbs

Adverbs, which describe verbs, are easily spotted because most of them end in *-ly,* such as *slowly, quickly, abruptly.* However, the adverb that causes the most errors is not a typical *-ly* form.

The adverb *well* is commonly confused with its adjective counterpart, *good.* As an adjective, *good* is used to describe nouns. In this sentence, *good* describes the noun *pasta:* The pasta you made last night was *good.* In the following sentence, *good* describes the verb *played,* which is incorrect: I played *good* in the basketball game. The correct word to use in such instances is the adverb *well.* Written correctly, the sentence would read, "I played *well* in the basketball game."

• Prepositions

Prepositions are connecting words that link a noun or pronoun to another word in a sentence. They are often used to show a relationship of space or time. For example:

The <u>box</u> *on* your <u>desk</u> is your birthday present.
The <u>holiday</u> that follows immediately *after* your <u>birthday</u> is Valentine's Day.

The first sentence uses the preposition *on* to describe the spatial relationship between the *box* and the *desk.* The second sentence uses the preposition *after* to describe the time relationship between *holiday* and *birthday. On your desk* and *after your birthday* are prepositional phrases.

COMMON PREPOSITIONS

aboard	at	between	inside	outside	until
about	before	by	into	over	with
above	behind	except	like	to	within
after	below	for	of	under	
among	beneath	from	off	up	
around	beside	in	on	upon	

The three most common problems with prepositions are:

1. **Using prepositions unnecessarily.** Because it is so important in your essay to get to the point concisely, unnecessary prepositions should be avoided. Remember that when two or more prepositions are used together, chances are at least one is unnecessary.

2. **Using the wrong preposition in a standard combination.** Certain words must always be followed by specific prepositions. These necessary prepositions are always used in combination with their respective supported words.
    Here is a list of several required prepositional pairings:

account for	*argue about*	*differ from*	*independent of*
agree upon	*compare to*	*different than*	*interested in*
angry with	*correspond with*	*identical to*	*speak with*

3. **Confusing *between* and *among*.**
    The third common mistake with prepositions involves the use of *between* and *among*. *Between* is used when talking about two things. *Among* is used when talking about more than two things.

● GOOF-PROOF EXAMPLE ●
TRICKY PREPOSITIONS

Poor form—I cleaned *up under* the kitchen cabinets.
Good form—I cleaned *under* the kitchen cabinets.

Poor form—She likes all sports *except for* soccer.
Good form—She likes all sports *except* soccer.

Poor form—They looked *outside of* the house for the lost cat.
Good form—They looked *outside* the house for the lost cat.

Poor form—The professor had to decide *between* giving a test, a quiz, or assigning a paper on *Hamlet*.
Good form—The professor had to decide *between* giving a quiz, or continuing our discussion of *Hamlet*.

Poor form—The work was divided *among* Luis and Joti.
Good form—The work was divided evenly *among* Chester, Luis, and Joti.

● GOOF-PROOF RULE OF THUMB ●
ENDING WITH A PREPOSITION

Of all the rules governing prepositions, none is more famous than: *Never end a sentence with a preposition!* While this rule holds true for many situations, it is not an absolute. It is perfectly acceptable to end a sentence with a preposition, especially if it makes the sentences flow better in your essay. For example, in popular speech, it sounds much more natural to say "That's all I can think of" than "That's all of which I can think."

The best technique for deciding to keep or remove prepositions at the end of sentences is to use your ear. What would the statement sound like if you kept—or dropped—the preposition? Does it sound like *you,* or does it sound like a college professor? Prepositions, like large thesaurus words, should not be used in an attempt to add importance or weight to your writing.

RULE #27: Avoid Dangling Participles and Misplaced Modifiers

Always avoid dangling participles and misplaced modifiers.

● **GOOF-PROOF IT!** ●

Dangling participles and misplaced modifiers, though sometimes difficult to recognize, are easily fixed by rearranging your sentence.

A *dangling participle* is a phrase or clause, using a verb ending in *-ing* that does not refer to the subject of the sentence it modifies. Since it is so critical that your reader understand your point easily and exactly, dangling modifiers (and indeed any ambiguous language) must be avoided.

● **GOOF-PROOF EXAMPLE** ●

Incorrect: While working on his English assignment, Tony's computer crashed.
—Was the computer working on the assignment?
Correct: While Tony was working on his English assignment, his computer crashed.

Goof-Proof Hint: Correcting a dangling participle involves adding and/or rearranging the words in a sentence to make the meaning clear.

Incorrect: While practicing outside with the soccer team, the noisy construction job distracted Jim.
Correct: While Jim was practicing outside with the soccer team, he was distracted by the noisy construction job.
Or
The noisy construction job distracted Jim while he was practicing outside with the soccer team.

A *misplaced modifier* is a word or phrase that describes something, but is in the wrong place in the sentence. It isn't dangling; no extra words are needed; the modifier is just in the wrong place. The danger of misplaced modifiers, as with dangling modifiers, is that they confuse meaning.

● GOOF-PROOF EXAMPLE ●

Incorrect: I had to have the cafeteria unlocked meeting with student government this morning.

—Did the cafeteria meet with student government? To say exactly what is meant, the modifying phrase "meeting with student government" should be moved to the beginning of the sentence.

Correct: Meeting with student government this morning, I had to have the cafeteria unlocked.

RULE #28: Nouns and Verbs Must Agree in Number

A singular noun takes a singular verb, and a plural noun takes a plural verb.

● GOOF-PROOF IT! ●

To achieve subject-verb agreement, first determine whether your subject is singular or plural, and then pair it with the correct verb form.

● GOOF-PROOF EXAMPLE ● AGREEMENT

Incorrect: Tim and Fran *is* a great couple.
Correct: Tim and Fran *are* a great couple. (Plural subject takes plural verb.)

Incorrect: One of my friends *are* going to your school.
Correct: One of my friends *is* going to school. (Singular subject takes singular verb.)

● GOOF-PROOF RULE OF THUMB ● AGREE TO DISAGREE

Agreement may be difficult to determine when the noun follows the verb. Common examples include sentences that begin with *there is* and *there are,* and *here is* and *here are.* When editing your work, remember to first determine whether your subject is singular or plural, and then match it to the correct verb.

Incorrect: There *is* too many meetings scheduled on Tuesday morning.
Correct: There *are* too many meetings scheduled on Tuesday morning.

Incorrect: Here *are* the report you asked me to write.
Correct: Here *is* the report you asked me to write.

● **GOOF-PROOF CHECKLIST** ●

The more complex the sentence, the more difficult it is to determine noun/verb agreement. Here are some guidelines to help you:

✓ If a compound, singular subject is connected by *and,* the verb must be plural. (Both the 10-speed *and* the hybrid *are* appropriate for the bike race.)

✓ If a compound, singular subject is connected by *or* or *nor,* the verb must be singular. (Neither the 10-speed *nor* the hybrid *is* appropriate for a trail race, however.)

✓ If one plural and one singular subject are connected by *or* or *nor,* the verb agrees with the closest subject. (Neither a fast bike *nor perfect trails are* going to help you to win if you do not train.)

[*QUIZ #7*]

Correct the following sentences, if necessary. The answers can be found in Appendix B on page 175.

1. My family and I is traveling to Spain.
2. Neither of your newsletter items were clearly written.
3. Both of the clerks is rumored to be fired after not showing up for work.
4. One of the pitchers injured his elbow.
5. Either you or your brother are going to have to talk to your parents.

RULE #29: Strive to Write In the Active, Rather Than the Passive, Voice

Not only is it clearer and more direct, but the active voice conveys your meaning more easily.

● GOOF-PROOF IT! ●

You will hear this unanimous piece of advice often: The active voice is much more effective in conveying your personality through your essay. You literally become the source of, or cause, the action.

If you use the passive voice, the subject (most often *you*) is acted upon. In addition, sentences written in the passive voice tend to be too wordy, or lacking in focus. The last thing you want in your essay is long sentences that are confusing to the reader. The good news is passive-voice errors are easy to omit from your writing.

● GOOF-PROOF EXAMPLE ● CHOOSE ACTIVE INSTEAD OF PASSIVE

Passive: Another helping was asked for by my friend.
Active: My friend asked for another helping.

Passive: My wallet was misplaced by me.
Active: I misplaced my wallet.

Passive: Three finalists for the open position have been selected by the administration.
Active: The administration has selected three finalists for the open position.

Goof-Proof Hint: Note the simplicity and directness of the second sentence in each pair. The first sentences, written in the passive voice, are clumsy and noticeably longer.

RULE #30: Avoid Verb Tense Shifts

Verb tenses must be consistent within each sentence and paragraph.

● GOOF-PROOF IT! ●

Unnecessary shifts from one tense to another not only sound unskilled, but may obscure meaning as well. For instance, when describing an event in the past, all verbs should be in the past tense. This seems like an obvious point, but tense shifts account for a large share of grammatical errors, and may be easily remedied.

● GOOF-PROOF EXAMPLE ●
TENSE SHIFTS

Incorrect: When we finished our lunch, we *decide* to take a walk.
Correct: When we finished our lunch, we *decided* to take a walk.

Incorrect: Last year the governor said he *is campaigning* for our candidate.
Correct: Last year the governor said he *would campaign* for our candidate.
OR
Last year the governor said he *was campaigning* for our candidate.

RULE #31: Avoid Double Negatives

As with verb tense shifts, the use of two negatives in a sentence not only sounds bungled, but it can also obscure meaning.

● **GOOF-PROOF IT!** ●

The advice here is simple: Use of double negatives is unnecessary and redundant. Eliminate it from your writing.

● **GOOF-PROOF RULE OF THUMB** ● **DON'T BE TOO NEGATIVE**

There are more negatives than just the obvious *no, not, never, neither,* and *nor.* Remember that *hardly* and *barely* are negatives, too. If you are using those words, you have a negative, so you do not need to double up.

● **GOOF-PROOF EXAMPLE** ● **DOUBLE NEGATIVES**

Incorrect: We *hardly never* see movies.
Correct: We hardly *ever* see movies.

Incorrect: There *aren't no* tickets left.
Correct: There aren't *any* tickets left.

Incorrect: Mary *doesn't* like *neither* of those books.
Correct: Mary doesn't like *either* of those books.

Incorrect: Vegans *don't* eat *no* dairy products *nor* meat.
Correct: Vegans *don't* eat dairy products *or* meat.

QUIZ #8

Correct the following sentences. If the sentence is correct, mark "correct." The answers can be found in Appendix B on page 102.

1. We barely didn't catch the train.
2. Lee didn't have nothing to say at the meeting.
3. Don't give up on your puppy; he just needs more training.
4. Heather never went nowhere on vacation.
5. I didn't know which book to consult.

RULE #32: There Is No Excuse for Spelling Mistakes

Spelling mistakes and the college admissions essay do not mix. Strive to improve your spelling skills, always use the spelling tools at your fingertips, and never knowingly send out an essay with a typo.

● GOOF-PROOF IT! ●

Spelling errors in your personal statement can be disastrous. The most original and otherwise well-written essays will make the writer appear careless, lazy, and unintelligent if they contain spelling errors. This is absolutely *not* the impression you want to give your reader. There is simply no excuse for even one spelling error in your essay.

Putting in a little time will improve your spelling quickly. You can learn and use the following simple spelling rules that cover the few dozen mistakes that account for the majority of errors. In addition, you can become a more proficient user of your computer's spell check feature. Last, give your essay to at least two good readers who will check for any spelling errors you may have missed.

● GOOF-PROOF GUIDELINES ● SPELLING RULES

● I before E

I before E except after C, or when sounding like A as in neighbor or weigh.

Though it has a few exceptions, this simple rule is worth remembering. The majority of the time, it works.

Exceptions:
After C: *ceiling, conceive, deceive, perceive, receipt, receive, deceit, conceit*
When sounding like A: *neighbor, freight, beige, sleigh, weight, vein, weigh*

Others: *either, neither, feint, foreign, forfeit, height, leisure, weird, seize,* and *seizure*

• Doubling Final Consonants

When adding an ending to a word that ends in a consonant, you double the consonant if:

1. The ending begins with a vowel (such as *-ing, -ed, -age, -er, -ence, -ance,* and *-al*).
2. The last syllable of the word is accented and that syllable ends in an single vowel followed by a single consonant (words with only one syllable are always accented). *Stop* becomes *stopping, stopped, stoppage,* or *stopper* because *stop* has only one syllable (so it is accented), and it ends in a single consonant preceded by a single vowel.

Here are some words that meet the doubling requirements:

run—running, runner
slam—slamming, slammed
nag—nagged, nagging
incur—incurred, incurring
kid—kidding, kidder
plan—planned, planning, planner
begin—beginning, beginner
set—setting
transmit—transmitting, transmittal, transmitted

• Dropping Final E's and Y's

When adding an ending to a word that ends with a silent *e,* drop the final *e* if the ending begins with a vowel, such as *advancing* and *surprising.*

If the ending begins with a consonant, keep the final *e,* as in *advancement* and *likeness.*

However, if the silent *e* is preceded by another vowel, drop the *e* when adding any ending: *argument, argued, truly.*

● GOOF-PROOF RULE OF THUMB ●
EXCEPTIONS TO THE RULES

To avoid confusion and mispronunciation, the final *e* is kept in words such as *mileage* and words where the final *e* is preceded by a soft *g* or *c: changeable, courageous, manageable, management, noticeable.* The word *management,* for example, would be pronounced with a hard g sound if not for the *e* after the *g.* If the root word ends with a silent *e,* and the suffix begins with a vowel, then take off the silent *e* and add the suffix.

come + ing = coming

If the root word ends with a consonant followed by the letter *y,* change the *y* to *i* and add the suffix.

reply + ed = replied

● GOOF-PROOF EXAMPLE ●
PLURALS

Most words are made plural by simply adding an *s.* However, if a word ends in *x* or *s, sh* or *ch,* the suffix *es* must be added to form a plural.

church/churches
box/boxes
plus/plusses

If the word ends in a consonant plus -*y,* change the -*y* into -*ie* and add an -*s* to form the plural.

enemy/enemies
baby/babies

Goof-Proof Hint: When in doubt, look up the singular form in the dictionary, where you will also find the plural listed.

• GOOF-PROOF EXAMPLE •
150 MOST COMMONLY MISSPELLED WORDS

1.	absence	32.	correspondence
2.	abundance	33.	deceive
3.	accidentally	34.	definitely
4.	accommodate	35.	dependent
5.	acknowledgment	36.	depot
6.	acquaintance	37.	descend
7.	aggravate	38.	desperate
8.	alibi	39.	development
9.	alleged	40.	dilemma
10.	ambiguous	41.	discrepancy
11.	analysis	42.	eighth
12.	annual	43.	eligible
13.	argument	44.	embarrass
14.	awkward	45.	equivalent
15.	basically	46.	euphoria
16.	boundary	47.	existence
17.	bulletin	48.	exuberance
18.	calendar	49.	feasible
19.	canceled	50.	February
20.	cannot	51.	fifth
21.	cemetery	52.	forcibly
22.	coincidence	53.	forfeit
23.	collegiate	54.	formerly
24.	committee	55.	fourth
25.	comparative	56.	fulfill
26.	completely	57.	grateful
27.	condemn	58.	grievance
28.	congratulations	59.	guarantee
29.	conscientious	60.	guidance
30.	consistent	61.	harass
31.	convenient	62.	hindrance

63. ideally
64. implement
65. independence
66. indispensable
67. inoculate
68. insufficient
69. interference
70. interrupt
71. jealousy
72. jewelry
73. judgment
74. leisure
75. length
76. lenient
77. liaison
78. lieutenant
79. lightning
80. loophole
81. losing
82. maintenance
83. maneuver
84. mathematics
85. millennium.
86. minuscule
87. miscellaneous
88. misspell
89. negotiable
90. ninth
91. occasionally
92. occurred
93. omission
94. opportunity
95. outrageous
96. pamphlet
97. parallel
98. perceive
99. permanent
100. perseverance

101. personnel
102. possess
103. potato
104. precede
105. preferred
106. prejudice
107. prevalent
108. privilege
109. procedure
110. proceed
111. prominent
112. pronunciation
113. quandary
114. questionnaire
115. receipt
116. receive
117. recommend
118. reference
119. referred
120. regardless
121. relevant
122. religious
123. remembrance
124. reservoir
125. responsible
126. restaurant
127. rhythm
128. ridiculous
129. roommate
130. scary
131. scissors
132. secretary
133. separate
134. souvenir
135. specifically
136. sufficient
137. supersede
138. temperament

139.	temperature	**145.**	usurp
140.	truly	**146.**	vacuum
141.	twelfth	**147.**	vengeance
142.	ubiquitous	**148.**	visible
143.	unanimous	**149.**	Wednesday
144.	usually	**150.**	wherever

● GOOF-PROOF RULE OF THUMB ●
USING COMPUTER SPELL CHECKERS

There is no reason to avoid using the spell check function on your word processor program. It's fast and simple, and catches many common spelling errors and typos. However, spell check is not foolproof. You should be aware of its three most important limitations, and rely on other methods to catch possible errors, especially for more important documents.

1. **Non-word versus real-word errors.** Most of us think of spelling errors in the first category, that is, a string of letters that does not make a real word. You might type sevn instead of seven, or th for the. Spell check is an excellent tool for catching these types of mistakes. However, if you are discussing the seven years of piano lessons you've taken, and you leave off the s and type even, spell check won't flag your error.

   This is known as a real-word error. You have typed a legitimate, correctly spelled word; it's just not the word you meant to type, and it doesn't convey the meaning you intended. Spell check can't find these types of errors.

2. **Proper nouns.** Spell check uses a dictionary that does not include most proper nouns and words in other categories, such as the names of chemicals. You can always add a word or words to the dictionary once you are sure of its spelling, but the first time, you will need to use another source (a reliable print one is best) to verify the spelling.

3. **Errors spelled similarly to another real-word.** If you misspell a word in such a way that it is now closer,

letter-by-letter, to a word other than the one you intended, spell check will probably offer the wrong word as a correction. For example, if your essay includes a coffee house scenario, and you type the word expresso, spell check will correct the error with express rather than espresso. Similarly, alot will be corrected to allot. You must pay careful attention to spell check's suggested corrections to ensure the right selection.

[*QUIZ #9*]

Can you spot the errors? Choose correct or incorrect by circling the appropriate term. The answers can be found in Appendix B.

1.	abundence	correct / incorrect
2.	basically	correct / incorrect
3.	collegiate	correct / incorrect
4.	existance	correct / incorrect
5.	fullfill	correct / incorrect
6.	globaly	correct / incorrect
7.	harrass	correct / incorrect
8.	lightning	correct / incorrect
9.	misspell	correct / incorrect
10.	ocassionally	correct / incorrect
11.	paralell	correct / incorrect
12.	possess	correct / incorrect
13.	questionnare	correct / incorrect
14.	receipt	correct / incorrect
15.	relavant	correct / incorrect
16.	scarey	correct / incorrect
17.	separate	correct / incorrect
18.	temperture	correct / incorrect
19.	vaccum	correct / incorrect
20.	whereever	correct / incorrect

RULE #33: Use Punctuation Marks Correctly

Punctuation allows you to convey certain tones and inflections, give emphasis where needed, and separate longer sentences into more easily defined and understood segments.

● **GOOF-PROOF IT!** ●

There are dozens of different punctuation marks in the English language; those covered in this section are the ones that present the most challenges to their users. While the information may seem simple, and has been taught to you numerous times during your education, it pays to review it. Not only will your writing be more polished and technically correct, but it will better convey your voice. Effective punctuation can therefore help you achieve the primary goal of the essay, revealing more of your personality.

● **GOOF-PROOF EXAMPLE** ●
THE APOSTROPHE

Apostrophes are used to indicate ownership. Eight rules cover all of the situations in which they may appear.

1. Add *'s* to form the singular possessive, even when the noun ends in *s:*

> The *school's* lunchroom needs to be cleaned.
> The *drummer's* solo received a standing ovation.
> *Mr. Perkins's* persuasive essay was very convincing.

2. A few plurals, not ending in *s,* also form the possessive by adding *'s:*

> The *children's* toys were found in every room of the house.
> The line for the *women's* restroom was too long.
> *Men's* shirts come in a variety of neck sizes.

3. Possessive plural nouns already ending in *s* need only the apostrophe added:

> The *customers'* access codes are confidential.
> The *students'* grades improved each semester.
> The flight *attendants'* uniforms were blue and white.

4. Indefinite pronouns show ownership by the addition of *'s:*

> *Everyone's* hearts were in the right place.
> *Somebody's* dog was barking all night.
> It was *no one's* fault that we lost the game.

5. Possessive pronouns never have apostrophes, even though some may end in *s:*

> *Our* car is up for sale.
> *Your* garden is beautiful.
> *His* handwriting is difficult to read.

6. Use an *'s* to form the plurals of letters, figures, and numbers used as words, as well as certain expressions of time and money. The expressions of time and money do not indicate ownership in the usual sense:

> She has a hard time pronouncing *s's*.
> My street address contains three *5's*.
> He packed a *week's* worth of clothing.
> The project was the result of a *year's* worth of work.

7. Show possession in the last word when using names of organizations and businesses, in hyphenated words, and in joint ownership:

> *Sam and Janet's* graduation was three months ago.
> I went to visit my *great-grandfather's* alma mater.
> *The Future Farmers of America's* meeting was moved to Monday.

8. Apostrophes form contractions by taking the place of the missing letter or number. Do not use contractions in highly formal written presentations:

> *We're* going out of town next week.
> *She's* going to write the next proposal.
> My supervisor *was in* the class of '89.

● GOOF-PROOF RULE OF THUMB ●
ITS VS. IT'S

Unlike most possessives, *its* does not contain an apostrophe. The word *it's* is instead a contraction of the words *it is*. The second *i* is removed, and replaced by an apostrophe.

When revising your writing, say the words *it is* when you come across *it's* or *its*. If they make sense, you should be using the contraction. If they don't, you need the possessive form, *its,* without an apostrophe.

⌈ *QUIZ #10* ⌉

Fill in the blanks with *its* or *it's* to complete the following sentences correctly. The answers can be found in Appendix B on page 176.

1. When _____ nice outside, Jorge enjoys hiking and camping.
2. Many people believe the big gas-guzzling car has seen _____ popularity dwindle.
3. _____ good form to send a thank you note after receiving a gift.
4. Store garlic in _____ own aerated container.
5. Janice feels _____ time to change her study habits.

GOOF-PROOF EXAMPLE
THE COMMA

Correct usage of commas is not as critical to the meaning of your sentences as it is with other punctuation marks.

Commas for Pace

Commas can be used to convey your voice as they speed up or slow down the pace of your sentences. Consider the difference in tone in the following examples.

During my junior year, I attended a conference in Washington, DC, in which student delegates from every state presented their ideas.

During my junior year I attended a conference in Washington, DC in which student delegates from every state presented their ideas.

The first sentence sounds more deliberate, giving a little more information with each clause. The second reads quicker, conveying the information faster and with equal weight on each part.

In addition to helping to convey your voice and personality, commas are often used misused. There are two common errors that all college-bound students should be aware of: the comma splice, and the serial comma.

Comma Splice

A comma splice is the incorrect use of a comma to connect two complete sentences. It creates a *run-on sentence.* To correct a comma splice, you can either:

- replace the comma with a period, forming two sentences
- replace the comma with a semicolon
- join the two clauses with a conjunction such as *and, because,* or *so*

Incorrect:	Our school received an award, we raised the most money for the local charity.
Correct:	Our school received an award. We raised the most money for the local charity.
Correct:	Our school received an award; we raised the most money for the local charity.
Correct:	Our school received an award because we raised the most money for the local charity.

• The Serial Comma

A serial comma is the one used last in a list of items, after the word *and*. For instance, notice the comma after *apples* is the serial comma:

At the store, I bought bananas, apples, and oranges.

The lack of a serial comma can cause confusion. In the sentence, *Cindy, Ann, and Sally were hired to work in the college counselor's office,* the message is straightforward. But if the serial comma is dropped, it could be understood as Cindy being told that Ann and Sally were hired. *Cindy, Ann and Sally were hired to work in the college counselor's office.*

While its use has been debated for centuries, the serial comma clarifies the meaning of sentences. Therefore, you should use it consistently whenever writing a list.

• GOOF-PROOF EXAMPLE •
COLONS

Colons appear at the end of a clause and can introduce:

1. a list when the clause before the colon can stand as a complete sentence on its own
2. a restatement or elaboration of the previous clause

Incorrect: The classes he signed up for include: geometry, physics, American literature, and religion.

Correct: He signed up for four classes: geometry, physics, American literature, and religion.

Incorrect: Shari is a talented hairdresser: she is also the mother of two children.

Correct: Shari is a talented hairdresser: she attends a seminar each month and has been a professional for over twenty years.

Colons have the effect of sounding authoritative. They present information more confidently and forcefully than if the sentence were divided in two other types of punctuation marks. Consider the following:

My teacher wasn't in class today: he had to fly to Houston to present a paper.

My teacher wasn't in class today. He had to fly to Houston to present a paper.

The first example, with the colon, has the tone that conveys, "I know why this happened, and I am going to tell you." It sounds more authoritative. This can be effective in your essay, but because you never want to appear pompous, it should be used sparingly.

● GOOF-PROOF EXAMPLE ●
SEMICOLONS

Semicolons may be used in two ways.

1. Use semicolons to separate independent clauses.

Case: Use a semicolon to separate independent clauses joined without a conjunction.

Example: Four people worked on the project; only one received credit for it.

Case: Use a semicolon to separate independent clauses that contain commas, even if the clauses are joined by a conjunction.

Example: The strays were malnourished, dirty, and ill; but Liz had a weakness for kittens, so she adopted them all.

Case: Use a semicolon to separate independent clauses that are connected with a conjunctive adverb that expresses a relationship between clauses.

Example: Victoria was absent frequently; therefore, she received a low grade.

2. Use semicolons to separate items in a series that contain commas.

Case: Use a semicolon to show which sets of items go together.

Example: The dates for our meetings are Monday, January 10; Tuesday, April 14; Monday, July 7; and Tuesday, October 11.

RULE #34: Use Capital Letters Appropriately

Capitalization is necessary both for specific words and to start sentences and quotes. Obey the rules of capitalization to ensure that your writing maintains the rules of punctuation.

• GOOF-PROOF IT! •

The six occasions that require capitalization are:

1. the first word of a sentence
2. proper nouns (names of people, places, and things)
3. the first word of a complete quotation, but not a partial quotation
4. the first, last, and any other important words of a title
5. languages
6. the pronoun *I*, and any contractions made with it

• GOOF-PROOF RULE OF THUMB •
PROPER NOUNS

Proper nouns require capitalization. Common nouns do not. How can you tell the difference? A proper noun is specific, referring to a specific person *(Stella)*, place *(Greece)*, or thing *(Honda Civic)*. A common noun is general, referring to a general group of people *(girl)*, place *(country)*, or thing *(vehicle)*.

[*QUIZ #11*]

Correct any capitalization errors in the following sentences. The answers can be found in Appendix B on page 177.

1. We are going to Portugal on vacation this summer.
2. Next wednesday is dr. lee's lecture.
3. Do you want me to pick up the copies at the xerox machine?
4. Kevin is learning Chinese in school this year.
5. Make a right on Maple st., and then stop in front of the post office.

● PUTTING IT ALL TOGETHER ●

No matter how great an idea you come up with, or how persuasively you can argue a point, an inability to express yourself clearly and accurately through the written word will hinder your success. Your writing must demonstrate that you are smart, accurate, and dependable because you are using proper grammar, spelling, and punctuation.

● GOOF-PROOF GUIDELINES ●

- Understand and avoid the common usage errors involving pronouns, adjectives, adverbs, and prepositions.
- A dangling participle is a phrase or clause, using a verb ending in -*ing*, that says something different from what is intended because words are left out. Since it is so critical to make the reader understand your point easily and exactly, dangling participles must be avoided.
- A misplaced modifier is a word or phrase that describes something, but is in the wrong place in the sentence. It isn't dangling; no extra words are needed; the modifier is just in

the wrong place. The danger of misplaced modifiers, as with dangling modifiers, is that they confuse meaning.

- Nouns and verbs must agree in number. A singular noun takes a singular verb, and a plural noun takes a plural verb. Determine first whether your subject is singular or plural, and then pair it with the correct verb.
- Strive to write in the active, rather than passive, voice. Not only is it more clear and direct, but the active voice conveys your meaning more easily. If you use the passive voice, your sentences may become too wordy, and lack focus. The last thing you want is long sentences that are confusing to the reader.
- Your use of verbs must be consistent. When describing an event in the past, all verbs should be in the past tense. Unnecessary shifts from one tense to another not only sound unskilled, but may obscure meaning as well.
- The use of two negatives in a sentence not only sounds incompetent, but it can obscure meaning.
- Spelling errors are unacceptable in your college admissions essay. Learn the Goof-Proof Spelling Rules to write error-free.
- Punctuation allows you to convey certain tones and inflections, give emphasis where needed, and separate longer sentences into more easily defined and understood segments. If you punctuate effectively, your essay will reveal more of your personality, a major goal of the personal statement.

section **SIX**

THE GOOF-UP:
NOT REVISING, EDITING, AND PROOFREADING YOUR ESSAY

Once you have a rough draft of your essay, you are ready to transform it into a polished piece of writing. This polishing process consists of three steps: revising, editing, and proofreading. Think of these steps as holding up various strengths of magnifying glasses to your essay.

Revising allows you to look at your essay through a lens that lets you see it as a whole; you will pay attention to the largest issues involved in its crafting. Have you addressed the topic? Is there a logical flow to your ideas or story? Is each paragraph necessary and properly placed?

Editing takes a closer look at your writing, through a stronger lens that highlights words and sentences. Are your word choices appropriate and fresh? Are there any repetitive or awkward sentences or phrases?

Proofreading puts your essay under the strongest lens. You will check *within* each word for errors in spelling, and also correct any other mechanics mistakes, such as grammar and punctuation.

You will also learn professional tricks to help you with revising, editing, and proofreading, such as finding and correcting mistakes using the power of word processors, and other ideas that help find errors that spell checkers might miss. Throughout Section Six, you will see model essays written by students who followed the Goof-Proof Rules and got into the colleges of their choice. In addition to the finished product, you will see how the revising, editing, and proofreading processes improved the original writing. The essays have been included here not to copy, but to show you how they work as a whole.

Many writers are tempted to skip the revising, editing, and proofreading steps, feeling intimidated by the thought of reworking their writing, and hoping their essays are good enough. If you follow the advice and procedures in the upcoming pages, you will learn how easy it is to polish your essay by following the Goof-Proof Rules. Many ideas can quickly improve the quality of your writing, even if you feel your rough draft is close to perfect. Remember, there is no excuse for submitting a personal statement that is not demonstrative of your very best writing.

RULE #35: How to Revise

From the Latin revisere, *meaning to visit or look at again, revision is the most general reexamination of your essay.*

● GOOF-PROOF IT! ●

The revision process can seem overwhelming. You need to look at your entire essay with fresh eyes, checking to see if you have achieved your goal, and if any sections of the essay need improving.

Here is the *Goof-Proof Strategy* for revision. First, put down your essay, and do not look at it for at least one day before revising. Next, read through it once, imagining you are reading it for the first time. Then, follow these steps in order to prepare your essay for editing and proofreading.

● GOOF-PROOF GUIDELINES ●

Read the following questions, noting that each numbered question correlates to a part of the sample "before" essay that depicts each particular issue. Then, read the revised "after" essay to understand how the writer fixed the problems. The two versions of the sample essay show the transformation writing undergoes during the revision process. You can refer to this exercise as a model for your own essay problem solving.

1. Does the content of your essay address or match the topic?
2. What does your essay say about you? Does it tell the admissions committee what they need to know?
3. Will your essay help you stand out against those who have similar grade point averages, class ranks, and test scores?
4. Is it memorable and interesting?
5. Would any reader understand everything you have written, or do some points need clarification?

6. Does the introduction have a good hook that draws the reader into the essay, or could it be eliminated?
7. Does your writing "flow?" Does it follow a logical progression, with each paragraph and point made in the right place?
8. Is your writing personal? Does it sound like *you*, or could someone else have written it?
9. Does your conclusion make sense after the preceding paragraphs? Is it strong, or just a wrap-up of what you have already said?

• Before

(6) <u>I want to be a teacher.</u> After all, throughout my life I had always worked with children. Every summer from eighth grade through high school, I worked as a camp counselor or a summer school teacher's aide. (7) <u>The camp that I worked at was in Colorado where the raging rivers and enormous mountains were a sight to be seen; a nature enthusiast's dream.</u> (2) <u>I always really loved children.</u> (8) <u>My interest in working with young people came naturally—I remembered how fun it was to be five years old, enjoying the learning process.</u>

(3)<u>Throughout high school, I have worked as a tutor at the Community Day School.</u> (4) <u>My favorite part of the week was "Mail Time." I created a fictional character—an elf named Mijo who lived in the room in which we met—to whom the children could write short, secret notes. It was both an exercise of their newly acquired and budding writing skills, and also an outlet for problems they needed to get off their chest. Through their</u>

notes, I also learned more about what they were going through. Once a week, the children would get individual notes in return from Mijo, with words of encouragement, little observances about their progress, or short anecdotes about rough times Mijo had in the past that mirrored the students' own experiences. Mijo even had his own signature notepaper and instead of signing his name, he drew a picture of himself. It was fun to get to know the children and to understand their worlds a little bit better; it's amazing what children will confide in an elf that they won't tell adults! As I got to know the students better, I was able to see what they needed to help them learn and grow.

When I was in elementary school, I always remember looking up to my teachers, and wanting to be in their position. (3) I am now working as a teacher's aide in an after-school program. Two aides had already quit because the students were so difficult; the class had already earned a reputation for being cruel. They relentlessly tease, name-call, and exclude one another. I also wanted my students to be exposed to a variety of learning encounters so that they could understand how their own complex environments affect their experiences, and how these experiences, in turn, affect their lives. (5) We analyze them by tricking them into playing games, but are really trying to make them better people. At this point, almost the end of the year, although they still have their difficult moments, my students are much more compassionate; they are learning to consider how their words and actions affect their peers. They are also learning how to communicate better, freely expressing and discussing their feelings so that they could resolve many of their own conflicts without adult intervention.

(9) I have discovered that, for me, the challenge of teaching is also the lure: that as the world changes, new questions, issues, ideas, and problems must be negotiated in the classroom. Students should have the opportunity to interact with and react to what they are learning in a way that is meaningful to them, and I want to be an active participant in this process. However, I think that in order to help them be actively involved in their own learning process, I need to formalize my knowledge and build a greater understanding of how kids learn, understand more about the relative strengths and weaknesses of different educational systems, and learn about philosophies of education in a program that addresses these issues. I want to know how students learn, what motivates an individual to learn, and most importantly how I can contribute to improving educational systems in my own community. I want to better understand the strengths and weaknesses of our educational systems so that I can foster and support a love of learning in young people and their teachers. Additionally, I want see the results of my work—I want to have direct contact with the learners I am serving.

• After

(6) <u>I am haunted by the question that plagues many upcoming graduates</u> . . . (1)what am I going to do now? Many of my friends and family members assumed I would become a teacher. After all, <u>throughout my life I had always worked with children.</u> Every summer from eighth grade through high school, I worked as a camp counselor or a summer school teacher's aide. (2) <u>I embraced every chance I had to be with children, and they in turn responded to my enthusiasm, energy, and the love of learning I shared with them.</u> My interest in working with young people came naturally—I remembered how fun it was to be five years old, proud of what I could read aloud, enchanted by my newfound abilities to create sentences and stories on paper, and so utterly fulfilled by counting to 100.

(3)<u>Throughout high school, I have worked as a tutor at the Community Day School. I worked with underserved first through third graders. I helped create lesson plans and designed educational activities to boost students' basic reading, writing, mathematics, and creative problem-solving skills.</u> (4) <u>My favorite part of the week was "Mail Time." I created a fictional character—an elf named Mijo who lived in the room in which we met—to whom the children could write short, secret notes. It was both an exercise of their newly acquired and budding writing skills, and also an outlet for problems they needed to get off their chest.</u> Through their notes, I also learned more about what they were going through. Once a week, the children would get individual notes in return from Mijo, with words of encouragement, little observances about their progress, or short anecdotes about rough times Mijo had in the past that mirrored the students' own experiences. Mijo even had his own signature notepaper and instead of signing his name, he drew a picture of himself. It was fun to get to know the children and to understand their worlds a little bit better; it's amazing what children will confide in an elf that they won't tell adults! As I got to know the students better, I was able to see what they needed to help them learn and grow.

When I was in elementary school, I always remember looking up to my teachers, and wanting to be in their position. (3) I am now working as a teacher's aide in an after-school program. Since my class already had a reputation for bad behavior, one of my goals from the beginning was for my students to understand more about their community—other teachers, each other, themselves, and me—so that they could become more aware of their own values and how their actions affect the world around them. I also wanted my students to be exposed to a variety of learning encounters so that they could understand how their own complex environments affect their experiences, and how these experiences, in turn, affect their lives. (5) We explore their social dynamics via a series of team-building games that provoke students to think about how their actions connect with and influence the world around them. At this point, almost the end of the year, although they still have their difficult moments, my students are much more compassionate; they are learning to consider how their words and actions affect their peers. They are also learning how to communicate better, freely expressing and discussing their feelings so that they can resolve many of their own conflicts without adult intervention.

(9) I have discovered that, for me, the challenge of teaching is also the lure: that as the world changes, new questions, issues, ideas, and problems must be negotiated in the classroom. Students should have the opportunity to interact with and react to what they are learning in a way that is meaningful to them, and I want to be an active participant in this process. However, I think that in order to help them be actively involved in their own learning process, I need to formalize my knowledge and build a greater understanding of how kids learn, understand more about the relative strengths and weaknesses of different educational systems, and learn about philosophies of education in a program that addresses these issues. I want to know how students learn, what motivates an individual to learn, and most importantly how I can contribute to improving educational systems in my own community. I want to better understand the strengths and weaknesses

of our educational systems so that I can foster and support a love of learning in young people and their teachers. Additionally, I want to see the results of my work—I want to have direct contact with the learners I am serving.

As you can see, the model essay has become tighter in scope and generally more appealing after the revision process. Now, start revising your essay by answering the questions from the Goof-Proof Guidelines, which will ensure that your essay follows the Goof-Proof Rules.

As you revise, be open to change. You may need to get rid of an anecdote and think of a better one. Don't get too attached to your anecdotes. While they may seem interesting and relevant to you, they could make less sense to objective third party readers. You may also need to delete a paragraph that is not relevant to and distracts from your point, or move paragraphs, sentences, and words to see if they fit better somewhere else.

Goof-Proof Advice from the Experts

By revising on the computer, it is simple to make changes, see if they improve the essay, and then save the changes (or try again if the change doesn't work). Don't be afraid to make necessary changes, and be willing to add and/or remove writing that isn't working toward the overall goal of a compelling, well-crafted, and focused essay. After all, you can always go back to the original version, which makes editing in a word processing program both less risky and more efficient. Take full advantage of the flexibility of word processing, and see Rule #37 for more word processing tips.

RULE #36: How to Edit

Editing your essay means checking, and improving when necessary, the words you have chosen, and the sentences in which those words appear.

● GOOF-PROOF IT! ●

Unlike revising, which entails the possible reworking of large parts of your essay, editing is a word-by-word and sentence-by-sentence task. While some students can do it effectively on the computer, you may want to consider printing out a hard copy to edit. Taking pen to paper may help you focus more closely on the pieces that make up your essay, rather than the work as a whole. Either way, the Goof-Proof Strategy for editing your essay involves carefully reading through each paragraph of your essay a number of times, paying close attention to the sentences and words that comprise them, and choosing the language that presents your ideas in the best possible manner.

● GOOF-PROOF GUIDELINES ●

Read the following questions, noting that each numbered question correlates to a part of the sample "before" essay that depicts each particular issue. Then, read the edited "after" essay to understand how the writer fixed the problems. The two versions of the sample essay show the transformation writing undergoes during the editing process. You can refer to this exercise as a model for your own essay problem solving.

1. Are all of your ideas and details necessary? Do they relate appropriately to the topic?
2. Do you repeat yourself? Rework your point so that you say it well the first time, and remove any repetitious words and phrases.

3. Do you have enough details? Look through your essay for generalities, and make them more specific.

4. Do you reinforce each point with a concrete and/or personal example?

5. Is your sentence structure varied? Sentences should not be the same length, nor should they be repetitive in any other way, such as all beginning with "I."

6. Are there any clichés or other types of overused language?

7. Do you use the active voice whenever possible?

8. Are there too many or too few adjectives and adverbs?

• Before

Most people associate the concept of a life partner with marriage. (1) <u>My parents have been married for almost 25 years, and we're planning an anniversary celebration for them next month.</u> My life partner and I have already spent seventeen years together. (5) <u>My life partner and I</u> shared a crib as infants as well as toys and tantrums as children. As teenagers, we have the typical disputes over driving and clothes and, in the future, will experience the challenges of adulthood together. My partner is not only my twin sister, but also my best friend.

My sister and I are completely different. (2) <u>No two personalities could be more different</u>. She is extremely artistic and introspective, and her unconventional sense of style commands recognition of her individuality. She tap dances, plays the flute, and writes for the school newspaper. I, on the other hand, am an athletic, outgoing person who enjoys participating in sports like soccer and basketball. I am very driven, a bit of a perfectionist, and am strict about maintaining organization. Nevertheless, these differences do not completely overwhelm our similarities. Katie and I love to laugh, are both determined and hard workers, and hold many of the same philosophical beliefs. The differing personalities she and I possess only help to strengthen our closeness.

I can trust Katie with anything because she knows all of my secrets—whether I tell her or not. We value each other's opinions and can depend on one another for support and encouragement. She is able to lighten the burden of my problems with her sarcastic sense of humor. Whenever I'm feeling down, she treats me to a movie or suggests we go shopping. My sister and I (6) <u>are like each other's shadows.</u> There is no one I would rather spend my time with.

Our relationship is far from perfect. We fight all the time and (3) <u>often become engaged in frequent arguments.</u> At the worst, these arguments may span for more than three days. (4) <u>She has problems that are discouragingly beyond my comprehension.</u> Anger results from my failed attempts to help her through them. (8) <u>The moods I experience at times create numerous conflicts as well.</u> Acceptance of our difficulties and at times temperamental attitudes, however, allow us to stick together.

(7) <u>Though we will eventually travel our own separate paths, the unique and sacred bond that</u>

exists between us will never be sacrificed by us. There is nothing deeper than the relationship of twins. It goes beyond even the parent-child relationship. Without question, my twin sister and I will always be there for each other. I will forever be grateful for the lifetime I have with her.

• After

Most people associate the concept of a life partner with marriage. My life partner and I have already spent seventeen years together. (5) We shared a crib as infants as well as toys and tantrums as children. As teenagers, we have the typical disputes over driving and clothes and, in the future, will experience the challenges of adulthood together. My partner is not only my twin sister, but also my best friend.

My twin sister, Katie, and I are completely different. She is extremely artistic and introspective, and her unconventional sense of style commands recognition of her individuality. She tap dances, plays the flute, and writes for the school newspaper. I, on the other hand, am an athletic, outgoing person who enjoys participating in sports like soccer and basketball. I am very driven, a bit of a perfectionist, and am strict about maintaining organization. Nevertheless, these differences do not completely overwhelm our similarities. Katie and I love to laugh, are both determined and hard workers, and hold many of the same philosophical beliefs. The differing personalities she and I possess only help to strengthen our closeness.

I can trust Katie with anything because she knows all of my secrets—whether I tell her or not. We value each other's opinions and can depend on one another for support and encouragement. She is able to lighten the burden of my problems with her sarcastic sense of humor. Whenever I'm feeling down, she treats me to a movie or suggests we go shopping. My sister and I (6) <u>are inseparable.</u> There is no one I would rather spend my time with.

Our relationship is far from perfect. We fight (3) <u>all the time about trivial things. I'm always complaining that she spends too much time in our shared bathroom, and she always accuses me of being impatient.</u> <u>My perfectionism also causes a lot of conflict between us because Katie thinks I'm trying to run her life when I make suggestions.</u> At the worst, these arguments may span for more than three days. (4, 8) <u>She has problems that I think could be easily solved, but when I'm unable to help her through them, I become frustrated.</u> Acceptance of our difficulties and at times temperamental attitudes, however, allow us to stick together.

(7) <u>Though we will eventually travel our own separate paths, we will never sacrifice our unique and sacred bond.</u> There is nothing deeper than the relationship of twins. It goes beyond even the parent-child relationship. Without question, my twin sister and I will always be there for each other. I

will forever be grateful for the lifetime I have with her.

As you can see, the model essay has become sharper and clearer now that corrections have been made in the editing process. Now, start editing your essay by answering the questions from the Goof-Proof Guidelines, which will ensure that your essay follows the Goof-Proof Rules.

Circle any problems or unclear areas as you encounter them. You might also make notes in the margin with an idea or two about how to improve the problem areas. After you have read through your essay a few times, and highlighted the areas that need improving, focus on one problem at a time. For example, if a point isn't made clearly and directly, or if it's too general, add a phrase or a sentence to clear it up, then move on to the next mark. Try not to get ahead of yourself or be intimidated by all the marks on the page.

Remember, the goal of editing is to make certain your essay works well on the level of sentences and words. By checking and correcting your writing closely, you can make you personal statement not only better focused, but more *personal*. As you eliminate words and phrases that don't work, you can simultaneously add details that clarify your writing and that also show the reader more about who you are. If you have followed the Goof-Proof Rules for editing, your essay will be fresh and original, with enough variation to keep your audience interested.

RULE #37: Professional Revision and Editing Tricks: Harnessing the Power of Your Word Processor

Afraid of making changes to your essay? It's easy when you know how to make your word processor function as a revising and editing tool.

• GOOF-PROOF IT! •

Making large and small changes to your essay may seem frightening at first: What if you don't like what you have changed, and want to go back to your original form? The directions in this rule show you how to use some of the many features of your word processing program to help you revise and edit. Follow the directions in this rule to free yourself from fear and try out variations on your essay.

In Rule #35, you were advised to use your word processor to look for areas that might be improved. In Rule #36, it was suggested that editing be done on a hard (paper) print out of your essay. Once you have completed those processes, and have an idea of the changes you want, or think you want to make, you can begin to add, delete, correct, and move text around. By using the *Track Changes* feature of your word processor, you can see what you have changed, and have the opportunity to save or undo your changes.

• Track Changes

Track Changes involves two different functions. One allows you to see what you are doing to the text as you revise and edit. The other lets you compare the "new" version to the original document. Therefore, the first step in using this feature is to copy your essay into a new document, creating a version that you can change and compare to the original (which is saved as a backup). To turn on the track changes feature, click on "Tools," "Track Changes," then "Highlight Changes." Select "Track changes while editing" and "Highlight changes on screen" to see the feature at work while you revise and edit. You may also want to check "Highlight changes in printed document" if you will work from a hard copy of your essay. "Highlight Changes" must be checked if you wish to see the changes tracked as you make them.

The next step is to choose how you want track changes to work for you. Open the "working" version of your essay, then click on "Tools," "Options," and "Track Changes." You will see four categories for which you can choose options. The following list explains each function.

Inserted text	An underline is the default. You may change it to bold, italics, or double underline. Choose a specific color (rather than the default "by author") to mark all inserted text in that color.
Deleted text	The default is strikethrough (a line going through the words(s) you remove). If you select Hidden, the deleted text can be shown or hidden with the Show/Hide button on the Standard toolbar. To prevent the deleted text from appearing on the screen, select the ˆ or # symbol.
Changed Formatting	"None" is the default. If you want to show any changes you make in formatting, select bold, italic, underline, or double-underline formatting.
Changed Lines	The default is outside border. Every paragraph that has a change shows a revision mark next to it. You can have these marks appear on the left, right, or outside borders.

Once you have revised and edited your essay, go back to the top of your document. Click on "Tools," "Track Changes" and "Accept or Reject Changes." Viewing options in this dialogue box are: Changes with highlighting," "Changes without highlighting," or "Original." You will be led to each change, with the option of accepting or rejecting it.

Examples of changes made with track changes:

My heart pounds wildly, (I can't believe no_one can hear it,) through the piano introduction, but with the first fphrase of the sweet melody, I loose myself in its beauty.

• Editing Options

Click on "Tools," click on "Options," and click on "Editing." There are eight editing options to choose, with the four options pertinent to your essay listed here.

Typing replaces selection	Turn this function on to highlight text to be removed, then type new text which will replace it
Drag-and-drop text editing	Perfect for moving words, phrases, and even paragraphs around in your essay. Highlight text to be moved, hold down left mouse button, move cursor to new location, and release the button to move the text.
Use smart cut and paste	Word automatically adjusts the spacing around deleted or inserted text when this function is on.
When selecting, automatically select entire word	Click once anywhere on a word to select the whole word.

• How to Select Text

To edit existing text you must first select the text that you would like to change. While everyone familiar with basic word processing functions knows how to highlight using the mouse, there are a number of ways to select text that can save you time, and prevent mistakes. To select:

- A single character: click and hold down the mouse button, then drag across the character.
- A single word: double-click on the word.
- One or more complete lines of text: move the cursor to the left side of the window until it turns into a right-pointing arrow. Click and hold the mouse button while dragging through the lines you want to select.
- A sentence: hold down the control key ("Ctrl"), and click anywhere within the sentence.
- A paragraph: triple-click anywhere within it, or move the cursor to the left side of the window until it turns into a right-pointing arrow and double-click.
- Multiple paragraphs: move the cursor to the left side of the window until it turns into a right-pointing arrow, double-click but hold down the mouse button on the second click. Drag up or down to select the desired paragraphs.
- A vertical block of text: hold down the control key ("Ctrl") and drag across the desired text.
- The entire document: move the cursor to the left side of the window until it turns into a right-pointing arrow and triple-click, or choose "Select All" from the "Edit" menu.

• How to Change Text

Once you have selected text, there are a number of ways to manipulate it.

To change text:
- begin typing new text; old will be replaced

To delete text:
- press the "Delete" key
- select "Cut" from the "Edit" menu

To move text:
- use the "Edit" menu to "Cut" or "Copy" the text. Next, click once at the desired location and select "Paste" from the "Edit" menu.
- hold down the left mouse button while on the highlighted text, and move the cursor to the desired location. Then, release the button. This is known as "drag and drop."

RULE #38: How to Proofread

The last step in the writing process is to correct every mechanics error you may have made.

● **GOOF-PROOF IT!** ●

Good proofreading involves far more than a simple run of the spell check and grammar check functions on your computer. In fact, those programs are far from Goof-Proof, and therefore a reliance on them alone to find your errors is a mistake.

However, these checking functions are not a bad place to start. Read the Goof-Proof advice for using spell and grammar check in Appendix A at the back of this book. Once you have made the corrections suggested by those programs, you will need to conduct checks of your own. Also, refer back to Rule #32 and review just what a spell checker can and cannot help you with.

The Goof-Proof Strategy for proofreading starts with a run of your spell- and grammar-checking functions. Then, after you have corrected your typos and usage mistakes, ask at least two other readers to look at your essay. Choose people you know to be good writers, who will pay careful attention when proofreading. Give each of them a fresh, goof-free, hard copy to work from.

Make another copy for yourself to use when proofreading, and consider these points. For your convenience, examples of potential goof-ups follow each number.

● **GOOF-PROOF CHECKLIST** ●

✓ Did you use any words incorrectly? (Check the lists of commonly confused and misused words in Rule #19 and Rule #20.)

> *Incorrect:* I researched *perspective* donors and prepared reports that aided board members in the selection of viable funding sources.

Correct: I researched *prospective* donors and prepared reports that aided board members in the selection of viable funding sources.

✓ When using quotation marks, did you place all sentence-ending punctuation inside of them?

Incorrect: My second summer of interning, I was involved in the Company's conversion process as they began their shift towards *"paperless audits"*.

Correct: My second summer of interning, I was involved in the Company's conversion process as they began their shift towards *"paperless audits."*

✓ Is there a good balance and proper use of contractions (not too few or too many)?

Incorrect: *I'm* committed to finding innovative solutions to the problems that prevent nations from achieving increases in productivity, ensuring quality healthcare for *it's* citizens and easing barriers to private enterprise. Specifically, *I've* an interest in finance and micro-enterprise development.

Correct: *I'm* committed to finding innovative solutions to the problems that prevent too many nations from achieving increases in productivity, ensuring quality health care for *its* citizens and easing barriers to private enterprise. Specifically, *I have* an interest in finance and micro-enterprise development.

✓ Do all subjects and verbs agree?

Incorrect: My *long-term goal are* to establish my own Hedge Fund.

Correct: My *long-term goal is* to establish my own Hedge Fund.

✓ Are there any double negatives?

Incorrect: Placing first in the state track and field championship 500-meter dash was *not no* easy task.

Correct: Placing first in the state track and field championship 500-meter dash was *not* an easy task.

✓ Have all hyphenated and compound words been used correctly?

> *Incorrect:* Through my work at various *nonprofit* organizations as a *high-school student,* I acquired skills in policy development and analysis, organizational management, and worked directly with low-income women and families.
>
> *Correct:* Through my work at various *non-profit* organizations as a *high school student,* I acquired skills in policy development and analysis, organizational management, and worked directly with low-income women and families.

Goof-Proof Advice from the Experts

Don't forget about checking headings and file names. If recycling your essay, make sure you state the appropriate school in your essay and as its file name. For example, make sure to change City University to State University when you send the same or modified essay to State.

See the next Goof-Proof Rule for even more help with catching errors.

RULE #39: Professional Proofreading Tricks to Catch Spelling Errors

Admissions officers expect your essay to have perfect spelling. Don't rely on spell check alone to catch your mistakes.

● **GOOF-PROOF IT!** ●

Here are a few professional proofreading tricks that can help you catch what your computer's spell check feature cannot.

● **GOOF-PROOF CHECKLIST** ●

✓ **Take your time.** Studies show that waiting at least 20 minutes before proofreading your work can increase your likelihood of finding errors. Get up from your computer, take a break or move on to some other task, and then come back to your writing.

✓ **Read backward.** Go through your writing from the last word to the first, focusing on each individual word, rather than on the context.

✓ **Ask for help.** A pair of fresh eyes may find mistakes that you have overlooked dozens of times, and one or more of your colleagues may be better at finding spelling and grammar errors than you are.

✓ **Go under cover.** Print out a draft copy of your writing, and read it with a blank piece of paper over it, revealing just one sentence at a time. This technique will encourage a careful line-by-line edit.

✓ **Watch the speed limit.** No matter which proofreading technique(s) you use, slow down. Reading at your normal speed won't give you enough time to spot errors.

✓ **Know thyself.** Keep track of the kinds of errors you typically make. Common spelling errors can be caught by spell check if you add the word or words to the spell check dictionary. When you know what you are looking for, you are more likely to find it.

● PUTTING IT ALL TOGETHER ●

Your essay is almost ready for submission. Before you send it out, be certain it contains no errors. That means taking the time to revise, edit, and proofread.

● GOOF-PROOF GUIDELINES ●

- Put away your essay for at least 24 hours before beginning the revision process.
- Read through your entire essay as objectively as possible. Is it interesting? Does it relate to the topic or answer the question?
- Check to see if your essay flows. Does it begin with a great introduction, move easily from one point to another, and end with an effective conclusion?
- Make sure your essay sounds like you, and tells the admissions committee what you want them to know.
- Don't be tempted to plagiarize another's words or ideas. Keep away from "free essays" and "essays for sale" websites and books.
- Print out a hard copy of your essay for editing.
- Check for ideas and details. Are there enough? Do they support your point?
- Make sure your writing is fresh. Eliminate repetition, clichés, and passive language.
- Use the powerful functions of your word processor to help you with revising and editing.
- Proofread your essay carefully for any errors in grammar, spelling, punctuation, and capitalization.
- Don't rely on computer spell check programs to find all of your mistakes. Follow the professional proofreading tricks to be certain your essay has no spelling errors.

THE GOOF-UP:
USING THE WRONG APPLICATION

Congratulations! Your essay is completed. You are ready to fill out your applications and send them in. Most schools now offer the choice of traditional hard copy or online submission. Even the hard copy admissions forms may be found online and downloaded, rather than ordered and sent through the mail.

If the school to which you are applying offers a choice of application forms, spend some time reading the instructions on paper and online to determine if they have a preference. You might find, for instance, that although a college still sends out paper applications, they state clearly on their website that online submission is preferred ("we encourage you to apply online"). Some schools even offer a financial incentive to do so, such as waiving or reducing the application fee for online submissions. Other schools require candidates to use a paper application if they seek entrance to a certain department (music, for example), or if they are applying to more than one degree program. Don't waste time by filling out one application only to discover that it won't be accepted, or that it is not the method of choice.

This section explains the benefits of online and traditional paper applications. You will learn the potential pitfalls of each, and how to avoid them, as well as tips to ensure your application looks its best, no matter which submission method you choose.

RULE #40: The Ins and Outs of Online Submission

More colleges and universities are offering the option of applying over the Internet. It has fast become the submission method of choice for many schools; but, it is not necessarily for everyone.

• GOOF-PROOF IT! •

The National Association for College Admission Counseling surveys its member each year to track trends in admissions. In 2002, 88% of colleges that responded reported an increase in electronic applications over the previous year and 76% of them reported an increase of between 1% and 40%, and 24% reported increase of over 40%. Why is there such a rise in online applications? There are two important reasons: They are easier for the schools and easier for the students.

Colleges and universities that accept online submissions appreciate the power of technology. Even schools that accept paper applications may scan them to create computer versions, and then shred the paper. The advantages of computerized applications are many. They may be sorted in countless ways, compared to one another, and compared with the school's admissions standards. Everyone in the admissions department can access and share all of the applications without photocopying or waiting for a file until it's their turn. This makes their job not only easier, but more time efficient as well.

Also, essays may be assessed by using anti-plagiarism programs and online searches.

Schools also like the online submission process because they find it is safe and secure. Applications can't get lost in the mail. As soon as you access an online application, your progress may be tracked, so the school to which you are applying knows when you have begun the process, when you have finished, and when you have submitted the application. For example, the University of Michigan's website asserts that "every submitted online application was received by our office last year with the data intact and loaded directly into our student information system, with the

Preview Portable Document Format (PDF) version available for UM personnel to review." As an added safeguard, when you apply online to any school, you receive an e-mail confirming the receipt of your application within 24 hours.

Many schools prefer online submissions to such a degree that they offer incentives to entice students to forgo paper applications. The following list represents many of the dozens of schools that waive their fee if you apply online. More than 10% of the colleges and universities that accept the common application are on the list. Since application fees can be as high as $70.00 each, the savings can be significant.

Albright College (PA)
Alfred University (NY)
Allegheny College (PA)
Arcadia University (PA)
Carleton College (MN)
Colgate University (NY)
Elizabethtown College (PA)
Emmanuel College (MA)
Guilford College (NC)
Hamilton College (NY)
Hartwick College (NY)
Hobart and William Smith Colleges (NY)
Hollins University (VA)
Hood College (MD)
Kenyon College (OH)
Le Moyne College (NY)
Loyola University (LA)
Manhattanville College (NY)
Marquette University (WI)
Randolph-Macon Women's College (VA)
Saint Norbert College (WI)
Salem College (NC)
Simmons College (MA)
Spring Hill College (AL)
Susquehanna University (PA)
University of La Verne (CA)

University of the Pacific (CA)
University of Rochester (NY)
University of Southern Maine (ME)
University of Toledo (OH)
Valparaiso University (IN)
Washington and Jefferson College (PA)
Washington College (MD)
Wellesley (MA)
Westminster College (MO)
Westminster College (PA)
Wheelock College (MA)
Willamette University (OR)
Wittenburg University (OH)

Other schools reduce the fee for online submissions, such as Albertson College of Idaho (ID) ($20.00 rather than $50.00), Boston University (MA) ($60.00 rather than $70.00), California Lutheran University (CA) ($25.00 rather than $45.00), Florida Southern College (FL) ($20.00 rather than $30.00), and Trinity University (TX) ($20.00 rather than $40.00).

Online applications are popular with students because they are easier to fill out and less time-consuming to complete. Since you are typing information on a computer, you don't have to worry about your penmanship, or about making errors that can look sloppy when corrected. Before filing your application, you can go back as many times as you wish to correct or edit your answers. Online submission also means no trips to the post office and no postage fees.

The capabilities of a few websites that offer access to hundreds of applications can greatly reduce the time spent on your applications, and make the process easier to manage. You select the applications you wish to fill out, and then enter information that may be saved from one session to another. On some sites, you can fill out a personal profile, which includes data such as your address, high school, and activities. The data is then automatically inserted in the correct places on all of your applications.

There are a small number of schools that offer applications online, but do not allow electronic submission. In other words, you may get a copy of the application on the Internet, and even fill it out online, but you must print it out and mail it when you are done. Less than 7% of the 230 schools that accept the common application require you to mail in the application rather than submit it electronically. While at first glance, this may seem unproductive, it is still advisable to use the online service for its ease and saving of time, and then print out the application(s) to mail in.

• GOOF-PROOF ONLINE ESSAY • SUBMISSION RESOURCES

Services differ; with some, you can fill out applications online, and save them (by creating an account which is password protected) so you can work on them a little at a time. Essays may be uploaded from your computer, and then the application may be paid for and submitted online. Other sites simply help you get either a hard or online copy of the application. Here is a list:

- www.app.commonapp.org (Common Application Online)—one application accepted by 230 schools. Many schools require a supplement to the common application; they are either available to complete and submit online, or may be found through a link to the school's website, where you can download and print the forms.
- www.collegelink.com—services include college and scholarship searches, test preparation, electronic college applications, and advice on paying for college. You can order either hard copies or Portable Document Format (PDF) applications.
- www.collegenet.com—offers more than 1,500 customized Internet admissions applications built for college and university programs. When applying to more than one program you save redundant typing since common data automatically travels from form to form. You can pay the admissions fees and submit applications online through the site.

- www.ecollegeapps.com—similar to collegelink; order applications online, then receive them electronically or via regular mail.
- www.princetonreview.com (formerly embark.com)—413 applications available. Research information available with the applications. Save time by filling out a profile; your personal information will be automatically inserted into each application you complete. You may also pay application fees and submit applications online.
- www.xap.com—almost 600 applications, scholarship and college searches, career information, and a high school planner. No general information entry; each application must be filled out individually.

  Xap.com also runs 29 "mentor" sites, most state-based, which provide online applications, as well as a confidential way to communicate with college in which you may be interested. You may also transfer data from your applications directly to the FAFSA (Free Application for Federal Student Aid).

• GOOF-PROOF CHECKLIST •

To submit an electronic essay, follow these steps:

- ✓ Find applications on one of the websites listed above, or download them directly from the schools' sites.
- ✓ Check deadlines and write them down. Create a timeline showing when you will complete each step in the application process, and when the completed application must be submitted.
- ✓ Order all necessary transcripts and test scores at least two to three weeks before you submit the application, so they arrive at about the same time as your application.
- ✓ If you are using the common application, check to see if the schools you are applying to require a supplement. If so, be certain to complete it. If the supplement isn't available through Common Applicaiton Online, you will need to

download it from the school's website, complete it, print it out, and mail it.

✓ Print out recommendation forms and distribute to those who will be filling them out. Include your resume or other form of information about yourself to help those completing the recommendations. An addressed envelope with proper postage, as well as a deadline reminder, are also necessary. Send out thank you notes to those who have completed recommendations for you.

✓ Follow instructions: They may require a certain font size and type, margins, or other formatting specifications.

✓ Check the application directions: Some essays are typed (or cut and pasted) directly onto the online application, while others take the essay as an attachment. If you are uploading, be certain you have formatted the document according to instructions.

✓ Fill out each application completely. Check any recycled parts of the common application or a recycled essay to be certain they refer to the correct school (you don't want to mail an application to Lehigh University that contains an essay about why you want to go to Lafayette!)

✓ Submit your application and pay any fees. (This may be done online or by a check through the mail—check directions.)

✓ Check your e-mail for confirmation that your complete application has been received.

RULE #41: The Ins and Outs of Mail-In Submission

There are a number of schools that require you to fill out a paper application and sent it to them through the postal service. Even if you are applying to a school that offers online applications, you may also prefer to submit by mail for a number of reasons.

● GOOF-PROOF IT! ●

You may be applying to a school or schools that do not accept online submissions; or, you may simply prefer to complete a paper application. In either case, you should be aware of the unique requirements of the hard copy application.

Goof-Proof Advice from the Experts

Dr. Beverly Lenny, a college counselor at Hunter College High School in New York, says she steers her students toward the paper application. Her main objection to the online version is her students' tendency to treat it casually. "The application process is about learning how to present yourself well. You must carefully show your readers your very best. The casualness with which some students approach online applications interferes with this sense of purpose."

Dr. Lenny's point should be thoughtfully considered. Do you tend to whisk off quick e-mails, attaching documents that may not have been carefully proofread? Do you think of online transactions as befitting casual relationships with friends? Will you be more careful and thoughtful with a paper application? If you honestly answer *yes* to any of the above, you should consider using a paper application, or at least be aware of the need to switch gears and approach the online application in a more professional mode.

There are a number of other reasons why you might decide to forego the ease of electronic submission and complete a paper application. If you are sending something with your application, such as artwork, recordings of music performances, or other supplemental material, you might want to package everything together with the paper application. This is the reason most often cited by students who choose the mail-in method. They prefer to put the total package together themselves.

● GOOF-PROOF RULE OF THUMB ●
PAPERWORK

Remember, the admissions committee will still need paper work that you cannot send yourself, such as recommendations and official transcripts. Another reason you might choose the paper application is the amount of space given for certain questions and answers. Depending on the application, online space could be less than what is allowed on paper. If you need more words to explain, for instance, why Scottish highland dancing is your most important extra-curricular activity, the paper application could be better for you.

Whether you choose to submit by mail or not, remember that the appearance of your application makes a statement about you. In other words, neatness counts. The biggest drawback of the paper application is the potential for a sloppy presentation: errors that are crossed out, smudges, typos corrected with globs of Wite-Out®. You won't get points for neatness, but you can lose out if your essay, and application as a whole, are messy.

● GOOF-PROOF CHECKLIST ●

To make your application the cleanest and most professional looking it can be, keep in mind the following:

✓ Print two copies of the application to use as rough drafts. Practice fitting in all of the information required in the given spaces. Use your rough draft as a model when you complete the actual application.

✓ Handwriting the application can lead to smudges, or errors that must be corrected with an eraser or wite-out. Use an erasable pen with blue or black ink, and test it to be certain it is flowing smoothly before writing on the application.

✓ Typing the application can make a neater appearance, but you must check for mistakes, and correct them as neatly as possible.

✓ You may combine both methods by handwriting basic information, and using a computer for answers that run more than a few words. Be sure the font size you are using will fit into the spaces on the application. Then, print out your answers, and literally cut and paste them neatly to the application. Alternately, if the school accepts copied applications, type and cut and paste everything, then make a clean copy to submit.

✓ Type your essay and any other information that is allowed to be submitted on another sheet of paper on the computer. Print it out after it has been edited and proofread, then attach it to your paper application. Note in the appropriate box that your "essay is attached."

✓ Be certain every page you submit has identifying information on it, such as your name and social security number.

✓ Take your time. Don't complete the real form until you have a finished rough draft. Slowing down and spending time practicing can significantly reduce the number of errors on your application.

✓ Make copies of your completed applications, in case any are damaged or lost in the mail.

● PUTTING IT ALL TOGETHER ●

When your essay in finished, you are one step away from sitting back, relaxing, and awaiting your acceptance letters. Most colleges and universities now offer two types of applications: traditional paper and electronic (online). If you have a choice, there are some important things to consider before deciding which type of application to use.

● GOOF-PROOF GUIDELINES ●

- Check the directions both online and on the paper application to see if the school has a preference or a rule regarding which you should use.
- If submitting online, check out some of the application websites that may make the process easier for you.
- Check deadlines and write them down. Create a timeline showing when you will complete each step in the application process and when the completed application must be submitted.
- Order all necessary transcripts and test scores at least two to three weeks before you submit the application, so they arrive at about the same time as your application.
- If you are using the common application, check to see if the schools you are applying to require a supplement.
- Print out recommendation forms and distribute to those who will be filling them out about a month before you plan to submit your application(s).
- Follow instructions: They may require a certain font size and type, margins, or other formatting specifications.
- Print two copies of the application to use as rough drafts. Take your time, and don't complete the real form until you have a rough draft to use as a model.
- Whether writing, typing, or using a combination of both methods on a paper application, check for mistakes, and

make any necessary corrections as cleanly as possible. Neatness counts!

- Be certain every page you submit has identifying information on it, such as your name and social security number.
- Check the application directions: Some essays are typed (or cut and pasted) directly onto the online application, while others take the essay as an attachment. Most paper applications note that your essay may be printed on an extra sheet of paper.
- Fill out each application completely. Check any "recycled" parts of the common application or a recycled essay to be certain they refer to the correct school.
- Submit your application with the correct fee. (Online submissions may be paid for through a secure server or by a check through the mail—check directions.)
- Make copies of your completed paper applications, in case any are damaged or lost in the mail.
- Check your e-mail if you submitted online; you will receive a confirmation that your application was received. If you sent in a paper application, you will receive a post card within approximately two weeks indicating it was received.

section **EIGHT**

RESOURCES

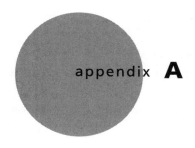

ONLINE AND PRINT RESOURCES, SPELL – AND GRAMMAR – CHECKING FUNCTIONS

• COLLEGE ESSAY RESOURCES •

The Internet has already made college application information readily accessible, and now we have cut your net-surfing time in half. You will find a variety of useful resources ranging from college application information websites to spelling, grammar, and general college admissions guides. If you prefer books to online materials, we have provided an ample list of related books, as well. Also, you will find quick, step-by-step summaries of various word processing techniques. Goof-Proof your research, and use these helpful resources to find the information you need to create your best college admissions essay.

• Online Application Websites

- www.app.commonapp.org (Common Application Online)—one application accepted by 230 schools. Many schools require a supplement to the common application; they are either available to complete and submit online, or may be found through a link to the school's website, where you can download and print the forms.
- www.collegeboard.com—apply to more than 500 universities online. Find the right school, organize your application process, and learn ways to finance your education.
- www.collegelink.com—services include college and scholarship searches, test preparation, electronic college applications, and advice on paying for college. You can order either hard copies or Portable Document Format (PDF) applications.
- www.collegenet.com—offers more than 1,500 customized Internet admissions applications built for college and university programs. When applying to more than one program you save redundant typing since common data automatically travels from form to form. You can pay the admissions fees and submit applications online through the site.
- www.collegeview.com—take virtual campus tours of over 3,800 schools, explore diversified campuses, register to win scholarships, and have specific schools personally answer your questions.
- www.ecollegeapps.com—similar to collegelink; order applications online, then receive them electronically or via regular mail.
- www.mycollegeguide.org—download the common application, hand pick your perfect school by region, cost, community, size, and type. Get advice and important information on the general college application process. Interesting articles on pressing issues that affect college-bound high school students.
- www.princetonreview.com (formerly embark.com)—413 applications available. Research information available with

the applications. Save time by filling out a profile; your personal information will be automatically inserted into each application you complete. You may also pay application fees, and submit applications online.

- www.xap.com—almost 600 applications, scholarship and college searches, career information, high school planner. No general information entry; each application must be filled out individually. Xap.com also runs 29 "mentor" sites, most state-based, which also provide online applications, as well as a confidential way to communicate with college in which you may be interested.

  You may also transfer data from your applications directly to the FAFSA (Free Application for Federal Student Aid).

● SPELLING AND GRAMMAR RESOURCES ●

● Spelling Websites

- www.dictionary.com—a useful online dictionary (with thesaurus). You can sign up for "word of the day" e-mails to help expand your vocabulary.
- www.funbrain.com/spell—a site designed for young people with a Spell Check spelling game.
- www.m-w.com—Merriam Webster Online. This site has a number of interesting features that will make you forget you are trying to improve your spelling! Check out the Word for the Wise section (www.m-w.com/wftw/wftw.htm) for fun facts about words.
- www.randomhouse.com/words/—Words @ Random. Here you will find crossword puzzles, quizzes, dictionaries, and other fun stuff all in one site.
- www.say-it-in-english.com/SpellHome.html—absolutely ridiculous English spelling.
- www.sentex.net/~mmcadams/spelling.html—this site has a tricky online spelling test that is worth taking.
- www.spelling.hemscott.net/—useful advice on how to improve your spelling.

- www.spellingbee.com/index.shtml—The Scripps Howard National Spelling Bee site contains "Carolyn's Corner" with weekly tips and information on spelling.
- www.spellweb.com—this site will help you to pick the correct spelling of two versions of a word or phrase.

• Spelling Books

Agnes, Michael. *Webster's New World Pocket Misspeller's Dictionary* (New York: Hungry Minds, 1997).

Devine, Felice Primeau. *Goof-Proof Spelling* (New York: LearningExpress, 2002).

Dougherty, Margaret M., et al. *Instant Spelling Dictionary* (New York: Warner Books, 1990).

LearningExpress. *1001 Vocabulary and Spelling Questions, 2nd Edition* (New York: LearningExpress, 2003).

Magnan, Robert and Mary Lou Santovec . *1001 Commonly Misspelled Words* (New York: McGraw-Hill, 2000).

Morrow, David. *DK Pockets: Spelling Dictionary* (New York: DK, 1998).

vos Savant, Marilyn. *The Art of Spelling* (New York: Norton, 2000).

• Grammar Websites

- http://eslus.com/LESSONS/GRAMMAR/POS/pos.htm—lessons on the eight parts of speech, with quizzes to reinforce material
- www.wsu.edu/~brians/errors/index.html—Paul Brians's "Common Errors in English" site.
- http://garbl.home.attbi.com/writing/—writing and grammar directory.
- http://iteslj.org/quizzes/—self-study quizzes for ESL students, but useful for anyone interested in grammar.
- http://babel.uoregon.edu/yamada/guides/esl.html—University of Oregon, Yamada Language Center Website

- www.protrainco.com/info/grammar.htm—the Professional Training Company's "Good Grammar, Good Style Pages."
- www.englishgrammar101.com—English Grammar 101. A pay service with a free trial that includes several English grammar tutorials.
- www.dailygrammar.com—daily grammar. This site offers daily e-mail messages with a grammar lesson five days of the week and a quiz on the sixth day. http://ccc.commnet.edu/grammar/—guide to grammar and writing.
- http://jcomm.uoregon.edu/~russial/grammar/grambo.html—a Test of the Emergency Grammar System.
- www.grammarbook.com—the popular Blue Book of Grammar and Punctuation online, with simple explanations of grammar and punctuation pitfalls, and separate exercises and answer keys

• Grammar Books

Follett, Wilson and Erik Wensberge. *Modern American Usage* (New York: Hill & Wang, 1998).

Fowler H. W., revised by Robert W. Burchfield. *New Fowler's Modern English Usage* (New York: Oxford University Press, 2000).

Johnson, Edward D. *The Handbook of Good English* (New York: Washington Square Press, 1991).

LearningExpress. *501 Grammar and Writing Questions, 2nd Edition.* (New York: LearningExpress, 2001).

Merriam-Webster. *Merriam-Webster's Guide to Punctuation and Style* (Springfield: Merriam-Webster, Inc., 1995).

O'Conner, Patricia T. *Woe Is I: The Grammarphobe's Guide to Better English in Plain English* (New York: Riverhead Books, 1998).

Olson, Judith F. *Grammar Essentials, 2nd Edition* (New York: Learning Express, 2000).

Princeton Review, *Grammar Start: A Guide to Perfect Usage* (New York: Princeton Review, 2001).

Sabin, William A. *The Gregg Reference Manual* (New York: Glencoe McGraw-Hill, 2000).

Scrampfer Azar, Betty. *Understanding and Using English Grammar* (New Jersey: Pearson, 1998).

Straus, Jane. *The Blue Book of Grammar and Punctuation* (Mill Valley: Jane Straus, 2001).

Strunk, White, Osgood, Angell. *The Elements of Style* (Needham Heights: Allyn & Bacon, 2000).

Wallraff, Barbara. *Word Court: Wherein Verbal Virtue is Rewarded, Crimes Against the Language Are Punished, and Poetic Justice is Done* (New York: Harcourt, 2000).

Walsh, Bill. *Lapsing Into a Comma* (New York: McGraw Hill, 2000).

Williams, Joseph M. *Style: Toward Clarity and Grace* (Chicago: University of Chicago Press, 1995).

● USING COMPUTER FORMATTING, ● GRAMMAR, AND SPELLING TOOLS

● Computer Formatting in Microsoft Word

Microsoft Word allows you to set everything from paragraph indentation to the look (font style and size) of different types of text.

1. Click on "Format" on the toolbar.
2. Click on "Style."
3. Find the "List:" box.
4. Click on "All Styles."
5. Scroll through the styles listed to find the item you wish to change.
6. Highlight the item by clicking on it.
7. Click on "Modify."
8. Click on "Format."
9. Choose what you would like to change (font, paragraph, etc.)
10. Make changes.

11. Click on "OK."
12. Click on "OK."
13. Click on "Apply."

• Computer Grammar Tools

You should always use a grammar check program on your writing. Grammar check can find possible errors, draw your attention to them, and suggest corrections.

The settings on these programs may be changed to check for only those elements that you specify; check for specific styles of writing, such as formal, standard, casual, and technical; and check for errors as you type, or when you are finished.

To modify the grammar check settings in Microsoft Word, open a blank document and:

1. Click on "Tools" on the toolbar at the top.
2. Select "Options."
3. Click on the "Spelling and Grammar" tab.
4. Click on "Settings" in the lower grammar section.
5. Read the list of options, and select those you want grammar check to look for.
6. Click on "OK."

Although you should always use grammar check, you should not always trust it. Grammar programs make mistakes, both by missing errors, and by flagging errors that are actually correct. In fact, there have been a number of studies done comparing the effectiveness of various programs, and they perform about the same (fair to poor).

The first problem, missing errors, is illustrated by the following examples. A grammar check on the following sentence did pick up the subject/verb agreement error (*I is*), but did not notice the participle error (*I studying*).

"I is ready to take the exam after I studying my notes and the textbook."

Similarly, the punctuation problems in the following sentence were not flagged.

"The recipe, calls for fifteen ingredients and, takes too long to prepare."

When grammar check does highlight an error, be aware that it may in fact be correct. But if your knowledge of grammar is limited, you won't know whether to accept grammar check's corrections. To further complicate matters, you may be offered more than one possible correction, and will be asked to choose between them. Unless you are familiar enough with the specific problem, this may be no more than a guess on your part.

While there have been improvements in computer grammar checking, nothing is more effective than a careful review of your writing after using the program.

• Using Computer Spell-Checkers

There is no excuse not to use spell check. It's fast and simple, and catches many common spelling errors and typos. However, spell check is not foolproof. You should be aware of its three most important limitations, and rely on other methods to catch possible errors, especially for more important documents.

1. **Non-word versus real-word errors.** Most of us think of spelling errors in the first category, that is, a string of letters that do not make a real word. You might type *sevn* instead of *seven,* or *th* for *the.* Spell check is an excellent tool for catching these types of mistakes. However, if a report you are writing includes information about the seven layers of management in your company, and you leave off the *s* and type *even,* spell check won't flag your error.

   This is known as a real word error. You have typed a legitimate, correctly spelled word; it's just not the word you meant to type, and it doesn't convey the meaning you intended. Spell check can't find these types of errors.

2. **Proper nouns.** Spell check uses a dictionary that does not include most proper nouns and words in other categories, such as the names of chemicals. You can always add a word or words to the dictionary once you are sure of its spelling, but the first time, you will need to use another source (a reliable print one is best) to verify the spelling.

3. **Errors spelled similarly to another real word.** If you misspell a word in such a way that it is now closer, letter-by-letter, to a word other than the one you intended, spell check will probably offer the wrong word as a correction.

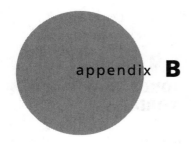

appendix **B**

ANSWER KEY

● QUIZ #1: LEARN THE MOST COMMONLY ●
CONFUSED WORDS, AND USE THEM PROPERLY

1. I *assured* my parents that I was making the right decision.
2. *Their* game was held last Saturday.
3. We enjoyed our trip to Boston better *than* our trip to Phoenix.
4. The *personnel* office is in the back of the building.
5. To *whom* should I address this letter?

● QUIZ #2: LEARN THE MOST MISUSED ●
WORDS, AND USE THEM PROPERLY

1. My brother was being indecisive, so I was forced to decide *between* the two movies.
2. After working long hours for three months, Joan was *eager* to start her vacation.
3. I lost the game but didn't *feel bad* because I'd tried my best.

4. Exhausted, she went to her bedroom to *lie* down.
5. The dinner *that* we ate last night was delicious.

• QUIZ #3: DON'T USE WORDS THAT •
AREN'T REALLY WORDS

1. He *brought* a calculator with him to the calculus final.
2. *I hope* the meeting will go well.
3. *Anywhere* you want to meet for lunch is fine with me.
4. *Regardless* of the weather, we are going to play golf.
5. People should take responsibility for *themselves*.

• QUIZ #4: DON'T USE WORDS OR PHRASES •
THAT MIGHT OFFEND YOUR READER

1. The chair*person* of our committee read a report regarding absenteeism among the wait staff.
2. Appropriate
3. The tennis players Venus and Serena Williams are the best in the world.
4. Please support the efforts of our Vice Principal, Dora Sinclair, by sponsoring her in the Relay for Life.
5. Did you send the invitation to Dr. Choe and *Ms. Jones?*

• QUIZ #5: UNDERSTAND POSITIVE AND •
NEGATIVE CONNOTATIONS TO
CHOOSE WORDS WISELY

1. *Inexpensive* has a positive connotation. Consider *cheap* to convey the idea negatively.
2. *Encourage* has a positive connotation; think of it in relation to *abet*.
3. *Aromatic* has a positive connotation; think of it in relation to *smelly*.

4. *Ludicrous* has a negative connotation; *amusing* is a more positive synonym.
5. *Cozy* has a positive connotation, whereas *comfortable* is more neutral.

● QUIZ #6: FORMALITY VERSUS INFORMALITY ●

Note that none of the formal words in this exercise are pretentious or archaic. You may create a more formal tone with simple words that get the point across.
Formal: *permit, eliminate, additional, unable to, assist*
Informal: *allow, get rid of, more, cannot, help*

● QUIZ #7: NOUNS AND VERBS MUST AGREE ● IN NUMBER

1. My family and I *are* traveling to Spain.
2. Correct
3. Both of the clerks *are* rumored to be fired after not showing up for work.
4. Correct
5. Either you or your brother *is* going to have to talk to your parents.

● QUIZ #8: AVOID DOUBLE NEGATIVES ●

1. We barely caught the train.
2. Lee had nothing to say at the meeting.
3. Correct
4. Heather never went anywhere on vacation.
5. Correct

• QUIZ #9: THERE IS NO EXCUSE •
FOR SPELLING MISTAKES

1. abundance
2. Correct
3. Correct
4. existence
5. fulfill
6. globally
7. harass
8. Correct
9. Correct
10. occasionally
11. parallel
12. Correct
13. questionnaire
14. Correct
15. relevant
16. scary
17. Correct
18. temperature
19. vacuum
20. wherever

• QUIZ #10: USE PUNCTUATION MARKS •
CORRECTLY

1. it's
2. its
3. it's
4. its
5. it's

● QUIZ #11: USE CAPITAL LETTERS ● APPROPRIATELY

1. No errors.
2. Next *Wednesday* is *Dr. Lee's* lecture.
3. Do you want me to pick up the copies at the *Xerox* machine?
4. No errors.
5. Make a right on Maple *St.*, and then stop in front of the post office.